The Legend of the
LUCKY LEE LOTT
HELL DRIVERS

Lucky Lee Lott

Motorbooks International
Publishers & Wholesalers ®

Acknowledgments

To my mother, Nellie A. Lott, December 12, 1880– September 2, 1983.

There were over 690 people connected with the production and presentation of The Lucky Lee Lott Hell Drivers show in its twenty years of existence. I am sorry that I cannot give credit to each and every one of them for their participation but here, in the course of my writing, I'll acknowledge their help and patience through the years. Thank you all very much. And thanks for your interest in my book.

A special thanks to all the others who have contributed help.

I close with this supplication from the land of Leprechauns, "May I be in Heaven a half hour before the Devil knows I'm dead."

Lucky Lee Lott

First published in 1994 by Motorbooks International Publishers & Wholesalers, PO Box 2, 729 Prospect Avenue, Osceola, WI 54020 USA

© Lee Lott, 1994

Motorbooks International is a certified trademark, registered with the United States Patent Office

Motorbooks International books are also available at discounts in bulk quantity for industrial or sales-promotional use. For details write to Special Sales Manager at the Publisher's address

Library of Congress Cataloging-in-Publication Data
Lott, Lee.
    The legend of the Lucky Lee Lott hell drivers / Lee Lott.
       p. cm.
    Includes index.
    ISBN 0-87938-858-7
    1. Lott, Lee. 2. Automobile drivers—United States—Biography. 3. Stunt driving—United States—History. I. Title.
    GV1032.L68   1994
    796.7'092—dc20   93-44775

On the front cover: Your faithful servant, Lucky Lee Lott, at work and at rest. The main image shows the Hell Drivers in action in 1953 doing our famous Dive Bomber stunt where we drove a car off a ramp and dove it into a junked car waiting below. The noise, smoke, and scream of tearing metal were all you could have hoped for. The inset photo shows me in Hell Drivers jodhpurs, leather boots, and football helmet alongside my 1953 Nash Ambassador Country Club stunt car. I never believed it when the newspapers described me as a miniature Gary Cooper. I just couldn't see it. I didn't smoke cigarettes and Gary did.

On the frontispiece: Hell Driver companions: Lucky Lee Lott, left, and Rocky Decker stand alongside the burning wreckage of a Head-On Crash at the Stratford, Ontario, fair in 1941.

On the title pages: A 1950 Nash Statesman restored and painted in Hell Drivers colors.

On the back cover: Once again, your servant at work and at rest. A motorcycle stunt and a car jump from the 1940s. The main image shows me in retirement wearing my civvies and standing next to my 1950 Nash.

Printed and bound in the United States of America

Contents

Foreword 1

By Richard B. Stolley

The Big Jump, 1939
The Los Angeles Coliseum played host to the largest Hell Drivers' show ever: 106,000 spectators. Here was our Nash stunt car in midair jumping so far that it cleared the 1924 Oakland catch car. That's me in the background along the fence crossing my fingers for a safe landing.

When I was only sixteen and the sports editor for the Pekin, Illinois, *Daily Times*, I wrote a front-page story about Lucky Lee Lott and his Hell Drivers. World War II was over, and gas rationing had ended. The Hell Drivers could roar again.

Lucky credits that story as being the first about his show. Knowing how famous the show eventually became, I find it hard to believe that I broke the news to the world. But since both Lucky and I were from Pekin, I am willing to take the credit on behalf of the small-town newspaper where I began my career.

Had I continued to report on Lucky Lee Lott, pursuing him and his exploits could have been a career in itself. He is truly one of a kind. This book tells you why—and in his own inimitable style. Heed his words: You can hear the bellow of his engines, you can feel the car break the bounds of gravity and soar breathtakingly and dangerously aloft, you can share the thrill and the heartpounding fear. In short, Lucky Lee Lott pulls you into his front seat and into his life.

And what a life it has been! You surely will say more than once as you read these pages, "Why, that damned fool is lucky to be alive!" Indeed, he is. You'll notice that Lucky is not just his *middle* name. But how fortunate we are that he lived to tell the gripping tale of how a young middle western daredevil conquered the globe.

Read and enjoy. But please, fasten your seatbelts—and never, never try these tricks yourself.

Richard B. Stolley
Senior Editorial Adviser
Time Inc.

Foreword 2

By Ivan "Fearless" Fosdick, Hell Driver

Ivan "Fearless" Fosdick
He earned his nickname.

Dear Lee: It's been thirty-nine years since I last saw you, but it seems as though it were yesterday. You were a good teacher when it came to stunt driving, and you also gave me a different view of life and what is expected of a man. I have always considered you as one of my best friends. In fact, if you needed, I would not hesitate for one minute to do all the crashes again.

I'm not much at this kind of thing, but I'll try to give you some of my remembrances of those times, our stunts, and our drivers. For all the world to know, I enjoyed the time spent with the Lucky Lee Lott Hell Drivers. It was a great experience—one not easy to forget.

One stunt you and I did together: The Double Rollover. We chained two cars together at the front bumpers, side by side. You rolled driver's side down and I rolled to the right. When the front ends came off the track from the roll—Lord, I don't know how high we went before we came down. After we landed, I remember looking for you through the windshield of my car and was more than thankful to see you move. You said, "That was enough of that." And you being the boss, I was more than happy to agree. I said to myself, "OK, Lee, got any more bright ideas?"

Do you remember the time we were ironing out a wet track with the cars? You were driving your town car and had the lady secretary of the county fair riding with you. Toothless was driving a stake truck with the clown car. When I drove past you—a little fast, I'll admit—my car threw mud all over your windshield, and my straight pipe must have sounded like a cannon to the secretary. When I came around again, you were in the grandstand gate laughing. Next time around I stopped to ask you what was so funny and you said the secretary had had an accident when I passed you. She was just in the wrong place at the wrong time.

And do you recall the time we were wiring the dynamite for The Dynamite Drive when a dog ran across the infield just as you were setting the charge. The dog hit the trip wire that touched off the charge while you were within 10 feet of it. The explosion and the aftermath! The Lord was with you that day, too, Lee. You could hardly hear for a long time. I know how we all felt when they took you away in the ambulance—a lot of nervousness and confusion was left at the track. A hard case of "The show must go on."

Lee, do you remember The T-Bone Crash you did when Fargo said, "Another one like that and you'll get your hearing back"? He were really angry about that one; he tried to slow you down but you wouldn't slow. The reason? Yep, I've got the reason—there's no excuse, just a reason. I was using a wood-and-cloth-topped Plymouth, so I had to hit it fast to go on through without flipping, but the bottom car was tough and I flipped anyway. I wound up with just the dashboard in front of me and the seat under me—the seat wouldn't have been there if I hadn't had the chain for the seatbelt running through the seat. There was no back to the seat when I stopped, no wheels, fenders, doors, or top, and I had flipped end over.

And there was another T-Bone Crash where you were so high in the air that you took down the horse-racing starter wire that was 18 feet off the ground. In fact, you came down on top of the wire. If the wire had been stronger, you'd have pulled the judges stand apart.

The dust was so thick that we couldn't see you and we were right on the racetrack. I ran to where you should have been and you were scrounging around through the floorboard. Finally you answered, "I can't find my glasses." But you did: they were broken in two. Walking back to the judges stand you said, "I think that helped my back somewhat, Fargo." That's when Fargo made the crack about you getting your hearing back.

That era was about the best time of my life. Even now, an old man, there isn't a day that passes that something doesn't come up reminding me of those escapades. To some it may mean nothing, but to me it's a part of my life, a part I loved and can never forget or can never get over. All the fellows, the crew, were like family. They'd come on the show and either fit or git. Later you coined the idiom, "Do it right the first time you're on; do it wrong the second time, you're gone." Everyone could depend on the man next to him.

You taught us that, Lee. You didn't have to tell us: we knew from watching you what was right and what was wrong. You were a silent teacher, undoubtedly the best I ever knew. You could take a man off the street who knew nothing of thrill show life and in one season he became a seasoned veteran. You never asked a man to do something you wouldn't or couldn't do yourself or that you hadn't done or wouldn't do yourself.

Long before I ever met you, Lee, I knew all about you. I had seen you and your show at county fairs and had also seen Fargo and Derby in action. When Kelly—Don Kelso, our announcer for several years—came to me with a proposition to join your show, I could hardly believe it. Kelly brought me down to Illinois for the show that very night. I quit my job hauling rock that minute, got into the sound car with Kelly, and we left for the show.

Fargo explained the routines to me, but he didn't tell me too much, just that I'd pick up on it by rubbing elbows with the guys and moving faster than the cars to get out of their way.

I made a mistake the very first night. Fargo explained the precision driving hand signals to pick up speed, slow down, hold it there, cut in, drop back, and so on; with crashes, you watched the track manager. I was scheduled for a crash roll. When I saw the roll ramps on the track, I forgot all about Fargo's lecture.

I knew nothing about the controlled rollover. I knew I was going to hit it but had no idea what was going to happen. I had upset a car a time or two but had never deliberately rolled a car before. I just accepted it as it came. It was a thrilling experience. I thought I had done a pretty good job, but then came Fargo's wrath. He yelled at me, "What the hell was the matter with you? Why didn't you watch me?" I answered, "No I didn't, but why? Did I do something wrong?"

He informed me that he was there to protect the spectators in the grandstand and along the fences, and the drivers must watch him for that reason. He might have had to turn me off because someone might be on the track that doesn't belong there. I had never thought of it in that manner, but after that I sure did. It was a lesson I never forgot.

We survived many of those crashes by the skin of our teeth. But as I said before, I would not hesitate to do all of the crashes again.

Ivan "Fearless" Fosdick
Hell Driver

> We survived many of those crashes by the skin of our teeth. But as I said before, I would not hesitate to do all of the crashes again.

The most Thrilling Show on Wheels!

"LUCKY"

LEE LOTT

PRESENTS

"LUCKY"

THE INTERNATIONALLY FAMOUS

"LUCKY" LEE LOTT

HELL DRIVERS

DAREDEVILS SINCE 1935 1952

Hell Drivers Program, 1952
This program was found in the "Car
in the Barn."

CHAPTER 1

17,981 Cars Laid to Eternal Rest

The fact is that I, Lucky Lee Lott, your faithful servant, laid to eternal rest 17,981 automobiles in my years as a daredevil driver. My life has been a Gasoline Opera of stunt car driving. I first entered the daredevil business in 1935 with a DeSoto Airflow and the group Satan's Pals. By October 1935, I changed the name and built the famous Lucky Lee Lott Hell Drivers.

My Hell Drivers crashed cars at state and county fairs in every town, city, village, and hamlet across the United States, as well as touring Canada, Cuba, Mexico, and South America. We performed from Alberta to Peru, Caracas to Los Angeles, as well as the Burning Privy Circuit, a string of small fairs that ganged together to hire us to play afternoons and nights in different towns. We stunted year after year on racetracks, football fields, and horse show arenas. If the thatch is getting white on your roof, you may remember my 1950 Nash daredevil cars painted in Pan American Red with my moniker on the side; I then had new Nashes in various other colors each year. And you may remember my stunts: The T-Bone Crash, The Human Jack, The Dynamite Drive, The Dive Bomber, The Flaming Walls, The Lake Jump, The Bus Jump, The Double Rollover, and more.

Those were the days when the automobile was the new kid on the block. People were thrilled and titillated to see speed and spectacle right before their very eyes. These were also the days before stunt driving was tamed as precision driving. In my time, I knew what the crowd wanted: Daredevil stunts followed by lots of smoke and tearing metal—and the driver emerging unharmed to bow to the crowd.

Perhaps you've heard my name buzzing around whenever some-

Lucky Lee Lott, 1953
Your faithful servant in Hell Drivers jodhpurs, leather boots, and football helmet alongside my 1953 Nash Ambassador Country Club stunt car. I never believed it when the newspapers described me as a miniature Gary Cooper. I just couldn't see it. I didn't smoke cigarettes and Gary did.

Barrel Wall Crash, 1939
A true Gasoline Opera: Plowing through flaming barrels in front of 98,000 spectators at Soldier's Field in Chicago as part of the Labor Day Wild West Rodeo and Thrill Show.

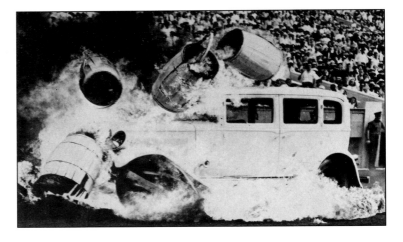

Dive Bomber, 1953
After the renown the Army Air Force and Navy dive bombers won fighting in the Pacific Theater of World War II, our dive bomber act grew in popularity—although Kamikaze may have been a better name. Hell Driver Jimmie Cook of Escondido, California, drove his car off a ramp at high speed and landed t-bone fashion into an innocent junker. What a stunt!

one mentions daredevil stunt driving—but I'd better get on with my pitch before you reach for the swatter. Please excuse me if you think I'm bragging but I must write down these living legends of the Lucky Lee Lott Hell Drivers that former drivers, friends, neighbors, and total strangers have brought forth to the gray matter.

If I don't tell it, it will never get told.

I was born a daredevil. At seventeen months of age, I crawled to the third story roof of an apartment building and refused to be rescued. I finally crawled back to safety under my own motive power when I had had enough. I did it my way.

At seventeen years of age, I dove from the tipple of a 218-foot-high bridge into the Illinois River, a stunt which I did again two weeks later for a magazine feature.

By the time I was twenty, I had formed the Satan's Pals mentioned earlier and embarked on a career as a stunt driver. This after various other "careers" as a door-to-door vacuum cleaner salesman, A&P grocery store flunky, circus trampoline artist, a high diver at the Chicago World's Fair, and the like. I don't have any war stories to tell, since I couldn't get into the service for World War II on account of the fact that I had wrinkled my back up in a 169-foot (35 feet straight up) world record leap with an automobile. I spent my war years in radio broadcasting, travelling with the Coca-Cola Spot Light Parade of Bands. I've also piloted airplanes through barns, decapitated automobiles under overpass bridges, stunted in many a Hollywood movie, hunted mountain lions in Tennessee, and enjoyed life all along the way.

True, other stunt shows tried to copy the Hell Drivers. But my stunt drivers could jump higher and crash harder than any of the

THE HELL DRIVERS
in action!

The Big Jump, 1946
A step-by-step lesson on how to do your own Big Jump stunt. First you get a ramp and line up a bus to jump over followed by four junkers to serve as a landing pad. You roar around the racetrack once to get up speed then over the ramp....

The Big Jump, 1946
...Bounce once onto the roofs of the crash cars....

The Big Jump, 1946
…Bounce again onto the final crash car, and then if you have too much speed….

The Big Jump, 1946
…You do a front flip and land upside down on the roof. This was Hell Driver Jimmie Cook at the wheel in Sioux Falls, South Dakota—and he got paid a bonus for doing that final flip. It isn't the going up that's rough, it's the coming down!

The Gang with Burning Car, 1941
The firemen had already left for supper when we completed this Head-On Crash in Stratford, Ontario. Each car was travelling at 60 mph when they hit—that's 120 mph aggregate speed. From left, clown Happy Maxwell, Rocky Decker, and Lucky Lee Lott. A job well done.

pretenders to the throne. As I said, I have laid to rest 17,981 cars—and crashed them in more ways than any other stunt driver. In addition, I totaled some 5,000 odd catch cars, which were nonrunning cars bought by our advance man from junkyards to serve as landing pads for our daredevils. I am still counting how many motorcycles and airplanes we demolished.

If you need any further proof, look in the 1951 *Webster's Collegiate Dictionary* under "Hell Driver": "A professional stunt man. Automobile acrobat." That's me.

If someone were trying to tell me the stuff that I have herein written, I wouldn't believe them. What proof? Well, to begin with, I have photos of a fair number of those 17,981 cars that I have totaled beginning in 1935 and a steady diet of crashes and crunches since. I have photos of almost every conceivable stunt that I ever pulled, including one of the dates where the Lucky Lee Lott Hell Drivers performed for 106,000 people at the Los Angeles Coliseum in 1939 and again in 1941.

I began in the 1930s crashing DeSotos and Model T Fords. I graduated in the 1950s to piloting Nash cars as Nash Motors became my sponsor. (No, the rumors you may have heard to the contrary, it is not true that I made the deal with Nash Motors because their cars would convert into beds so that my men could introduce bedroom fantasies to the fair country maidens.) I even once bought a 1923 Pierce-Arrow for $10, used it for The Board Wall Crash, a Brick Wall Crash, a Rollover, and then as a "catch car" for a stunt car to land on top of after completing The Bus Jump—and then sold it for $10 to the groundskeeper in Toledo, Ohio, who was still driving it five years later as a pickup truck. That was part and parcel of the Lucky Lee Lott Hell Drivers, and I'm mighty proud of it.

And then there were the motorcycles and airplanes. I liked Indian Scouts the best, as any Wall of Death or Motordrome rider will tell you. The pinnacle of my motorcycling career was the time I rode a cycle through a sheet of 28-gauge furnace metal, the first Tin Wall Crash ever.

Airplanes are another story. I was infamous for my outlawed Airplane-House Crash, which was best done with a Stearman biplane but which I also performed to immense personal satisfaction with a Ford Tri-Motor.

Did Lucky Lee Lott know what he was doing?

Well, I'm writing this book at age 78. I must have had an inkling.

I'm not about to apologize for what has passed as my way of life. Having been born of the astrologic sign of Taurus the Bull, I've assumed all the traits consistent with that sign; namely, stubborn, bull-headed, set in my ways, domineering, but at the same time I am decreed to be bland, loving, expansive, and contented and yet am supposed to be the "balance wheel" for the rest of the Zodiac. The stars carry some augury of the things to come.

All of this you the reader will ascertain if you will be so kind as to follow my writings and the stories of those who have kept the Lucky Lee Lott name in the back of their memory bank and brought forth at this time memories of my past good, bad, and indifferent so that the woven web will not be all deceiving to you, good reader, nor disparage from any preconceived ideas you may or may not have had of me.

As I said, if I don't tell it, it will never get told.

Wanted!, 1950
My advertising flyer for fair booking agents. Aliases included "Producer of the Impossible." The US Post Office made me redo this flyer because it looked too real.

CHAPTER 2

Born a Daredevil, or How I Got My Nickname

Pekin Bridge
The Illinois River bridge at Pekin where I first stepped off into national fame in 1931 with a 218-foot gainer dive from the wheel platform. They tore down the bridge in 1983. When asked recently if I could still do that dive, my retort was, "You put the bridge back, I'll do the dive." *Dean Zehr/ Pekin Daily Times*

I have fond recollections of my very first daredevil stunt. It was 1917 and I was seventeen months old. I was with my grandmother visiting her dear friend Mrs. Temple who lived in a three-story brownstone. It was July and since there was no air conditioning in those days, people left their doors and windows open. Since my grandmother and Mrs. Temple were busy chatting, I left to reconnoiter. I managed the doors alright and I climbed the stairs going up. All the way up.

I was discovered—or rather undiscovered—after a half hour. This was enough time to manipulate the step that led out a front dormer window onto the roof. Little Lee Lott was sitting astride the gable of the dormer looking down at those tiny people looking up at him. What fun for a seventeen-month-old child. Thirty feet in the air.

The fire engine arrived with a blaring siren. I had a toy fire engine at home with a ladder just like the one down in the street. Then they started to scream at me and that's when I got excited. I didn't like that: They wanted me to stay there until someone came up and got me. Oh, no, I was going to do it my way. I knew even at that tender age that I couldn't do it the quick way. I'd better go back the way I came up.

That I did. I carefully manipulated the rungs of the ladder around the corners and reached for the window when Mrs. Temple stuck her long, bony arms out and grabbed me.

A star was born to the daredevil world—and a well-paddled star at that. My exploit earned me my nickname Lucky as it was agreed all around that I was lucky I didn't fall. I knew better: I loved heights from that day forward.

**Portrait of the Daredevil as a
Young Man, 1946**
Flyer for county fair booking agents
promoting "The World's Greatest
Daredevil."

Program, 1942
On our way to becoming stars,
here's a program from the "Wild
West Rodeo & Thrill Circus" that
played the International
Amphitheater in Chicago. Slotted in
between the Lone Ranger and trick
roping, we performed all of the
greats from The Battering Ram to
The Dive Bomber before the fat lady
sang "God Bless America."

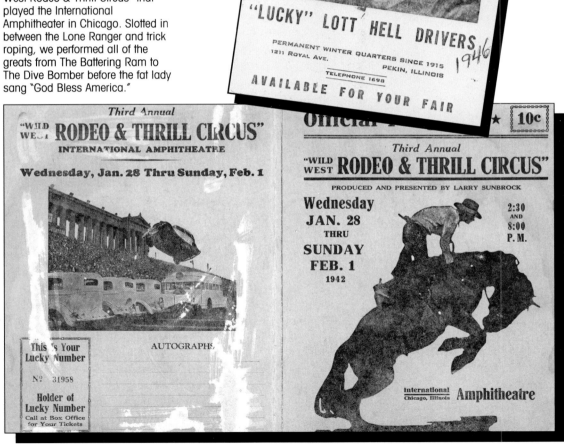

"THE WORLD'S GREATEST DAREDEVIL"

"Lucky"
Lee
Lott
Features
His

"LUCKY" LOTT HELL DRIVERS

PERMANENT WINTER QUARTERS SINCE 1915
1211 ROYAL AVE.
PEKIN, ILLINOIS

TELEPHONE 1698

1946

AVAILABLE FOR YOUR FAIR

Third Annual
"WILD WEST **RODEO & THRILL CIRCUS**"
INTERNATIONAL AMPHITHEATRE

Wednesday, Jan. 28 Thru Sunday, Feb. 1

This Is Your
Lucky Number

Nº 31958

Holder of
Lucky Number
Call at Box Office
for Your Tickets

AUTOGRAPHS

Official ★ 10c

Third Annual
"WILD WEST **RODEO & THRILL CIRCUS**"
PRODUCED AND PRESENTED BY LARRY SUNBROCK

**Wednesday
JAN. 28
THRU
SUNDAY
FEB. 1
1942**

2:30
AND
8:00
P.M.

International
Chicago, Illinois **Amphitheatre**

I came by it honestly. My father, Leonard Guy Lott, was a railroad brakeman and my mother, Nellie A. Lott, was a turnverein gymnast performer. It was my mother who taught me showmanship.

I was preceded by four years by a sister and two years by a brother, Rea, and then there was me. Mom thought she had her family all organized until six years later almost to the day, along came Neal Lott, who would later go into hell driving under my tutelage before setting up his own show in Canada.

Dad railroaded on the New York Central with Grandad Lott who engineered the sixteen-wheel locomotive behemoth on which my dad was brakeman.

My dad once saved a baby's life from the cow catcher. He and fellow railroader Gene Waechter were riding the toe board, a resting place on the front of the steam engine where brakemen ride to hook up cars. Up ahead they saw a baby crawling between the rails with the 98-ton locomotive barreling down on it. There was no time to stop the train. With Gene holding his belt, dad reached out and grabbed the only thing the babe was wearing—its diapers. At 25 mph, he only had one chance, and he pulled the babe to safety.

My dad later lost his life under a railroad coal car because the yardmaster and inspector did a slipshod job of maintenance inspection on the rolling stock. He had been thrown between two boxcars and dropped to the rails under the wheels. His body was mangled, but he raised his arm and helped himself off the rail until Grandad stopped the train after traveling about thirty feet. Grandfather's fireman had seen dad thrown off the car and under the wheels.

My father lived nine hours after the murderous incident. He had twenty-one breaks in fourteen ribs, both lungs were punctured, and his skull was fractured. He was still able to talk to his family and never lost consciousness.

Dad's death left nothing but a mortgage, funeral expenses, and four kids to feed. The railroad said, "Tough luck." I was eleven years old.

To help the family earn money to live on, my older brother Rea, a high school freshman, carried newspapers on a daily basis, and he also had a push cart to collect bottles, metals, paper, and the like.

One bright afternoon after school let out, Rea was headed for the *Pekin Daily Times* to pick up his eighty-two newspapers for delivery. A block from the high school was an intersection called Five Points, which was ungoverned by traffic lights as was typical in that day and age. By the witness of the other kids in the area, Rea had plenty of time to cross the street, but the driver of a Model T Ford decided to swerve from his own, right side of the street. He drove to the opposite side of the street and into the oncoming lane heading for my brother, from all indications, to scare him. Rea already had his back to the traffic lane he had left and the Ford hit my brother with the left fender, picked him up, tossed him into the air, and threw him against an old-fashioned cast-iron horse-watering trough, which was still necessary in the 1920s. In throwing him, it spun him around so that his head hit the steel with the base of his skull. He lived for four days without regaining consciousness.

Rea's paper route, and earning much of the family's income, became my burden.

With things the way they were at home, I had to try to earn an income. I was thirteen years old and there didn't seem to be any spare time beyond work. Over the next several years, I got jobs as a newspaper delivery boy, a runner for the town's German Bakery, an A&P flunky, a door-to-door vacuum cleaner salesman, and more.

In my thirteenth year, I also started on the road that would eventually lead me to run away with the circus. An adult friend of the family, Benny Wells, built a trampoline and I became a gymnast with his help. Benny didn't have the wherewithal to build a show piece, but he did, however, have the intestinal fortitude to go for something he liked.

Benny got some old telephone poles and made a form, 10 feet wide and 15 feet long. He secured the corners and laid the frame over a 3-foot-deep hole in the ground. To this frame, we added strips of old automobile inner tubes. These strips were 6 inches wide and when cut in one continuous strip could be 30 feet long. We wove the strips together, attaching them side by side and tacking them to the end rails. We then used shorter pieces and laced them over and under, crosswise, plaiting the whole of the "bed," after which we secured the plaiting with strips of wood.

With a wide belt about my waist attached to safety ropes and Benny on the other end, I had no qualms about doing the flips high in the air. I could bounce on the bed and soar sky high at 65 pounds. I could fly into the air and turn over like a yo-yo. Or by turning my head with a jerk, I could flip and twist at the same time. It seemed that I possessed an innate ability to know my positions in turning and spinning, or both, at the same time. It was easy for me to change revolutions and direction in mid-flight.

In 1927, my mother gave me permission to join the Seil-Sterling Circus out of Wisconsin. She had been a trapeze artist in her

My exploit earned me my nickname Lucky as it was agreed all around that I was lucky I didn't fall.

Side-by-Side Stunt, 1950
Two Nashes roar off the ramp side by side and drive on two wheels down the North Vernon, Indiana, county fair track. Yes, this is what I dreamed of doing from a young age—although I did promise my mother I would retire from daredevilry at age 40.

early days, so she was not afraid of my running away with the circus as most mothers would be. I left with Benny as my guardian.

Those were the golden years of the classic old circus. The whole crew lived on a circus train and we travelled throughout the midwestern United States from Minnesota to Indiana, stopping to set up our big tents with the elephants pulling the poles into place and the roustabouts pounding in the stakes with sledgehammers. Our entourage consisted of the ringmaster, a complete musical band, wire walkers, trapezists, trampoline acrobats, magicians, animal trainers, clowns, and all the rest that go into making up the biggest show on Earth. We were accompanied by our Noah's Ark of elephants, lions, tigers, dogs, and ponies.

The circus performer that made the greatest impression on me was a magician, Howard Thurston. Few people probably remember him as he didn't have the acclaim of Houdini or Blackstone. The Great Thurston worked on the circus sideshow as an illusionist, and taught me a lot about performing. If you want to learn the trick behind the illusion, don't watch the magician's right hand waving in the air for all to see; watch his left hand pulling the dove out of his pocket.

My second stunt brought me back full circle to my first stunt—except magnified by my years of experience in between. I had been seventeen months old then; I was seventeen years old now.

There was a guy who had a mighty fine speedboat, a mahogany-hull Dodge. We would cruise the Illinois River at speed while I did tricks on his aquaplane surfboard that he pulled behind.

One day we were riding under a new railroad bridge that was being built at Pekin to span the river. I told my buddy to meet me with his boat at noon next Sunday under the bridge.

The next week, I went to Sunday school and wore my swimsuit under my Sunday clothes. That was in the days of one-piece swimsuits that covered the chest. I didn't say anything to anyone and got out of church and walked over to the bridge. The watchman was just pulling away with his lunch pail on his bicycle handlebars.

I snuck onto the bridge. The railing was as high as my head so I could hide behind it as I walked all the way out to the center of the steel span. Making sure that I wouldn't be noticed, I had to go clear across the lift span to the other side where 190 steps led to the top. I took off my clothes and shoes and wrapped them into a bundle and tied them to a rope I'd brought along. I lowered the bundle down to within a foot of the water and tied it off. I scampered up the steps, steel ribs hard on my bare feet. I had a mission to accomplish.

I got to the top platform and sat down to catch my breath. The place was dead quiet, with no one around. I sat against the wall on the top platform to get my wind, looking out over the whole state of Illinois from my vantage point. I had never been that high up in my life, but I loved it. I loved anything that sparked with risk.

Suddenly, sirens were wailing everywhere. Holy cow! I jumped up as the police car drew up to the fence across the bridge. The chief of police and another officer jumped out and started to run up the approach. How did they know I was here?

I was not about to let them take me back down those steel steps on bare feet.

There being no railing at that height, I toed the edge, took a deep breath, and stepped out into space. It was like walking up a wall to go into a "gainer" dive—that's a back flip forward. I did about five gainers on the way down, because that type of dive will slow one down and a person can control his dive by using the method.

Just as I left the platform I heard a familiar sound, a speedboat under the bridge, idling.

I dove 218 feet, cut into the water, and quickly pulled up before hitting the river's bottom. Mission accomplished. What a thrill!

My buddy swung his boat around while I went over to where my clothes were in the bundle on the piling. We acted like we didn't know each other. He kept talking real loud to me, telling me I shouldn't have done that and all that stuff.

The policeman hollered down for him to take me over to the Court Street landing by the fish market. The police were friends of my father when he was alive, and I could see the mischievous pride in their eyes. They let me have it, just like my father would have tied into me.

My mother was the one who was really proud when she heard of the stunt.

In 1933, I began getting paid for my high diving. I was hired at the Chicago World's Fair to do two diving stunts: 120 feet into 10 feet of water and 75 feet into 3 feet of water, twice a day at the Streets of Paris. In 1934, I was back for the second year of the Chicago World's Fair, A Century of Progress.

Being nineteen at the time, I was a small-town kid who grew up fast in the two summers at the Windy City. I met people like Fred Astaire, Lew Ayres, Joe E. Brown, Sophie Tucker, Eddie Cantor, Dan Durea, and my old friend The Great Thurston.

Like the saying goes, I did it my way and never got hurt.

If you want to learn the trick behind the illusion, don't watch the magician's right hand waving in the air for all to see; watch his left hand pulling the dove out of his pocket.

CHAPTER 3

A Show Is Born: Satan's Pals

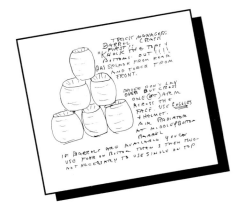

Barrel Crash Plans, 1935
My original sketch for Satan's Pals stuntmen indicating how to do the crash successfully. As my notes read, "Driver don't lay over but cross one (left) arm across the face. Use goggles and helmet."

I had a stash of loot from selling vacuum cleaners and so I decided to spread my wings and get into the daredevil business.

I didn't have a resumé to handle such endeavors as stunt driving but I did have other qualifications, to wit: I was a salesman—for evidence look at my vacuum cleaner savings. I could act in front of people—wasn't I with the circus at one time? I liked to do daring things—consider the roof stunt at seventeen months of age, my bridge dive at seventeen years, and my high diving at the Chicago World's Fair. And I had a gift of gab. Who needs a resumé with qualifications like that?

So Lou "Batter" Crooks, sundry other buddies, my fourteen-year-old brother Neal, and I got together around the kitchen table and began plans. It was 1935.

The first thing was a name. Satan's Pals sounded pretty spooky. We could have cars painted white like a ghost from the cemetery highlighted by red-colored signs like fresh blood. Well, let's not get carried away, but it was a step in the right direction.

I knew an old-timer in the nearby town of Washington who was in the auto junk business. He might just be able to "promote" a car or two for show cars. I'd look into it.

Satan's Pals with Lucky Lee Lott at the head of the gang. Had a certain ring to it. He's twenty something years old, drives a fancy new car, one of those DeSoto Airflows that he bought with his high-diving earnings. He can draw pictures and print signs that won't quit, signpainter for the Mackinaw Cheese Company, you know.

Satan's Pals. A daredevilry stunt show full of chills, thrills, and spills. We would play every county fair in the state of Illinois. It was just what the fans wanted—even though they didn't know it. Yet.

Satans Pals got under way.

The next morning, Ike Bluemenschein and I made a deal for two 1935 Fords, a Tudor and a Fordor that had been wrecked, one rolled and the other half burnt out from a backseat fire. The top was burned out of the two-door, whereas the doors of the four-door would not open from the roll. Batter opened the driver side with a bodyworker's tool (a 16-pound sledgehammer). He then got his welding kit out and permanently shut the other three doors as well as placing 1 1/2-inch reinforcing pipes at each doorpost and around the roof. This was going to be the "roll car."

So we started practicing. I had gotten permission from a farmer named Soldwedel to use his field to practice, and we turned many a

Flaming Board Wall Crash, 1935
Satan's Pals in action—with the crowd at a safe distance. This was an early show at Janesville, Wisconsin.

fast lap around that pasture.

One of the first rolls we did earned us an instant degree from the school of hard knocks. My young brother Neal did a rollover in an ancient Graham car. He had a 6-foot-long piece of baling wire as a safety belt wrapped for his own protection in a leather jacket. Batter decided to ride shotgun while the fourteen-year-old, six-foot one-inch Lott took to the wheel. The wire across his lap, Neal piloted the Graham, swerving the car from side to side, first left and then right, until the right front wheel dug in and the car rolled. In fact, the car rolled twice, once with both guys, once with only one guy. On the second flip, Batter's door flew open and without a bailing-wire belt to hold him in, he wound up on the ground. He spent the next week with the high collar of his coat tight around his neck, but he got over it, saying, "That's like doing a high dive without any water in the pool."

In truth, doing stunts like that without ramps was like a carpenter building a house without a hammer. So, during nights, I was at the drafting board (our kitchen table) designing a set of ramps and blocks for jumps; the design I created in those first days of Satan's Pals remained the exact design during my full tenure of

Satan's Pals, 1935
The first two daredevil stunt cars owned and operated by Satan's Pals parked in front of my home and office at 1211 Royal Avenue in Pekin, Illinois. In the foreground was my DeSoto Airflow painted ghostly white with blood red lettering announcing a show on July 24, 1935. As the rear wheel cover promised, there would be "Thrills, Spills & Free Parking."

daredevil business for the next twenty years.

Each of the Pals had the opportunity to try their hand with the roll car in practice. That poor vehicle suffered—oh, how it suffered! With Batter as our mechanic, we took all the tools we could scrounge out to Soldwedel's field to keep the cars alive, everything from pliers to screwdrivers to our trusty sledgehammer.

We collected lumber off of scrap billboards to build ramps and walls to crash through. I had a little money saved, so I bought the gas and bologna.

People gathered from miles around to watch these strange go-ings-on. Some were so fascinated they even donated cars for us to practice on.

We had a method, and so now my motivation was to get some-where to debut the show.

A daredevil show like Satan's Pals couldn't get onto a fairgrounds or racetrack because I didn't have an insurance policy backing me up. So I took a ride way out a hundred miles and found an air-port at Kewanee, Illinois, and made a deal for the Fourth of July with the airport man for use of the field for 25 percent of what we took in. Done deal.

I set up shop, had posters and handbills printed, and found a junkyard that would let us have six cars for $1.25 each (that's one dollar and twenty-five cents apiece). The junker even delivered the cars out to the airport on the first of July.

And then trouble came a calling. Someone got to palavering with the manager, who then demanded an insurance policy. There wasn't time to get one, even if we had had the money. A thousand dollars, no way!

That was a predicament. Two days before show date and we couldn't get onto the grounds. (I learned a lesson about contracts and by the next week I had one written, but it was too late for the airport show.)

I was standing around at the airport cursing my woes when I looked across the road and saw a farmer on top of a little rise work-ing on a fencepost. I piled out of my DeSoto and climbed the little hill to introduce yours truly and shake hands. I asked him if there was a pasture, track, or something somewhere where I could rent to put the show on for the Fourth of July. His name was Thomas and he said, "What's wrong with this right here?"

I took a few steps forward and looked across at a seven-acre pas-ture, over a quarter-mile long and 500-feet wide. A miniature of today's dragstrip.

I had a stash of loot from selling vacuum cleaners and so I decided to spread my wings and get into the daredevil business.

Lucky Lee Lott, 1935
Yours truly at age twenty when I organized the debut of Satan's Pals.

"Perfect," I realized and we made the deal. Farmer Thomas said that we didn't need a contract, that a handshake was good enough. He was to get 25 percent of all the money we'd take in, and his wife, son, and daughter would help sell tickets.

I dashed into town, got a roll of dimes and quarters to use the pay phone, and started to call the newly formed Satan's Pals, man by man. It was noon and the first thing the crew had to do was get Batter out of bed. You did that by pulling the mattress onto the floor and then throwing water into his face.

It was two days before show date.

The paint was dry on one Ford, the four-door roll car, but not on the other so we would have to get by without the two-door. We needed to get the show set up and it was going to take the full forty-eight hours to do it.

I had my own public address system, so I attached it to the DeSoto and made the rounds of the surrounding area for 40 miles, telling everyone of the show "opposite the airport" in Kewanee.

All we needed now was binder twine and pieces of cloth to control the crowds and lay out a race course in the pasture. The crew got to work and we hauled the cars over from the airport across the road. I had brought along a roll of 500 tickets, which we hoped to use all of. Kids were free.

I had a portable typewriter and worked on things to say, jokes and that sort of stuff. I didn't want to forget the commercials for the people who bought newspaper space and had their names on our advertising: the local shops for Standard Oil, Goodyear Tires, and the like.

The crew had everything in order. We lay down in the shade of the junkers and sacked out. We had put in some hard labor.

The day of the show arrived. The farmer's family came over and I gave them nail aprons packed with tickets and change money and they went off over the rise to the highway to handle something they knew nothing about.

The show was set for 2 pm. I had music on the turntable at 1:00, and there we waited, hoping someone would come see us. Our site being in a small valley, we naturally couldn't see the highway in either direction but heard a horn once in a while.

At 1:30, I looked up and here came an Illinois Highway State Trooper walking across to my car.

Oh, no!

"Who runs this outfit?" Bull Moose asked.

My voice never cracked as it did on the Fourth of July 1935.

"I'll have to take the blame, but we're waiting for customers."

Bull Moose responded, "If you'd open that gate, I'll help you get them in."

What?

"You've got a backup of traffic four miles to the light in Kewanee and five miles down to Route 91. Let's get with it."

I called my brother to help with the traffic and we ran for the gate to the field. It wasn't even open! The farmer's family had thought that I was going to come out and take tickets.

That didn't happen.

Route 34 was a national route and four lanes at that. It was packed with cars as far as the eye could see. But the cars weren't blocking the traffic—everyone was headed for the show.

The 500 tickets didn't last long. "Just take the money," I called out to our crew and the farmer's family, all working feverishly to get the crowd into the pasture. The farmer said, "How will we know

The "Ugly Five," 1935
The original cast of Satan's Pals taken during practice days at Soldwedel's field before our first show. From left, Lucky Lee Lott, Lou "Batter" Crooks, Blassey Aque, fourteen-year-old Neal Lott, and Jess Aque. Among our stunts, Blassey did a back flip from one moving motorcycle to another. Jess did a Human Battering Ram board wall crash while strapped to the hood of the DeSoto (and earned a splinter through his cheek when he looked up too soon). After our maiden run to Kewanee, Illinois, the Aques never travelled with the show outside of Pekin appearances.

how much there is?"

"We'll count it and deduct the change."

It took us an hour to get all the cars inside.

"You're going to run out of space," the trooper observed.

I turned to farmer Thomas. "How much will that patch of soybeans pay you after you harvest?" I asked.

"That's about an eighth. Probably $50–$60."

"OK, I'll buy it for $60 and you won't have to harvest it. Deal?"

We shuttled the balance of the cars into the soybean field.

I put the "Comedian's Gallop" record on the turntable and got the show in action at exactly 3 pm with apologies to all.

We kicked off the first Satan's Pals show with The Two-Wheel Drive. I drove my DeSoto onto a ramp and lifted two wheels off the ground, piloting it the length of the pasture. We did The Slide For Life with a daredevil hanging off the rear bumper, sliding along behind the car at 50 mph through a patch of burning gasoline.

Ramp Plans, 1935
My original plans for the ramps, which we ended up using throughout the days of Satan's Pals and the Hell Drivers.

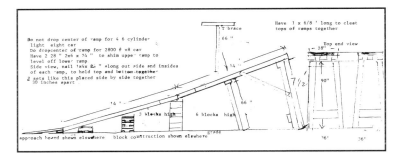

Blindfold Jump Preparation, 1935
Whitey Young blindfolds Vern Rupert at a Jackson, Michigan, show of Satan's Pals. The blindfolded Rupert would ride his Harley-Davidson off a ramp and through a burning board wall. Whitey was one of the clowns of the show's early days.

Then The Human Battering Ram with our man laid head-forward on the hood of the Ford while another drove him through a board wall set aflame. Batter did a motorcycle board wall crash along with some precision driving. And there was The Ski Wall where a car was jumped off a 2-foot-high ramp and through a blazing wall.

The finale was to be a head-on collision and the cars were a 1926 Dodge sedan and a Kissel Speedster, one of the boat-tail cars similar to an Auburn of the time. Built about 1922, the Kissel was a two-seater with left-hand steering, and no one would volunteer to do the driving from the front seat, even at 20 mph.

Batter agreed to try chauffeuring the Dodge from the rear seat at 20 mph. That would be a 40 mph aggregate speed crash.

A volunteer for the two-seater was chosen. Lucky Lee Lott.

Driving the Kissel in the head-on crash was a matter of driving from the right-hand side with both feet propped on the dashboard. I tied a rope around my chest and over the tonneau, and another half-inch rope across my waist and back to the rear bumper bracket on the right side to pull me away from the steering wheel. Batter's Dodge was controlled by a wire to the throttle and the Kissel's gas pedal was under my left foot.

The front bumpers were removed from both cars and we figured to meet with the right wheel of each car in the middle of the other's radiator. We each had an eighth-mile run.

Ready. Aim. Fire.

My car was sluggish, but Batter's Dodge scattered sod getting under way because he let it all hang out. The head-on crash would take place in the center of vision for the standing spectators.

One word describes that crash for me: "Oof!" We aimed, we travelled, and we *oof*ed! Boy, what a jolt, about 25 mph apiece.

In view of the severity of it, I thought I'd literally "bust a gut."

Batter had laid back in the rear seat after he'd taken aim when we were about 20 feet apart and placed his feet on the middle of a sturdy set of Dodge Brothers front seat cushion tops. That position gave him leverage so that he would vault over the top of the seat, which he did, and right through the top of the fabric-covered car. At which point, getting hit like a sparring partner in the boxing ring, I thought I'd bust a gut laughing. He dropped back into the car in a daze.

And the crowd was pleased as well. Chills, spills, and thrills.

After the show, it took a long time for the people to leave the premises and we had a lot of cleaning up to do. The junk man was on tap to first grab his batteries and radiators and then start the

One of the first rolls we did earned us an instant degree from the school of hard knocks

process of taking the wrecks back to Kewanee.

It took us until 9 pm that night to get things straightened out. The pasture had to be raked so the farmer could turn his cows out the next morning. The farmer's soybeans could still be used and they wanted us to come back the next year. The state trooper accepted a $30 donation for the "fraternity"; there were six officers at the show before it was over with and they all loved it.

I was as happy as a clam. Satan's Pals were no longer amateurs. We had lost track of the crowd at 500 tickets and so we went on to charge $1 a car. After advertising and printing, farmer Thomas' pasture rent as well as the soybean field, and all other expenses were paid, Satan's Pals had netted $980. We were in business!

We had totaled six cars in that first show. Little did I know but I had 17,975 cars to go before calling it quits!

After the first show of the Satan's Pals, we stayed over at the farmer's field. We couldn't drive the 80 miles home because we had one headlight out on the DeSoto and no headlights at all on the 1935 Ford sedan. We camped on the grounds where we had performed, sleeping under the stars.

Having made $980 clear that day, I had no idea what to do with the money, so I dug a hole and buried the cash and backed the Airflow over the cache.

In the morning, we took off for Pekin and home. We felt like returning gladiators. Six kids in a business of our own. A dream we were sure going to see blossom.

The first factors I knew I was going to have to deal with were professionalism, regimentation, continuity. I didn't know what that meant but it sounded good. Especially for a young bunch.

I found enough white shirts and ties to go around, and the guys wore whatever they had on for trousers. A couple of us had invested in jodhpurs and riding boots. We had football helmets (2) and aviator helmets (4) to make it look professional.

For that first date out, we had rigged a two-wheeled trailer over a tubular axle so we could haul our stunt cars. We built the ramps and blocks of my own design—none like it were ever seen—and I used the design all the years of my stunt work. In fact, later on when we first played Philadelphia, a novice race car driver who was trying to turn daredevil sneaked onto the racetrack at Yellow Jacket Speedway attempting to photograph my equipment and get the measurements of the same. We ran the bum off.

Satan's Pals was a good bunch of guys. There was good conduct, nothing wild about the bunch, no grandstanding with exuberant actions by individuals. Perhaps that's where my Taurean stubbornness came in and drew the resentment of some of our performers. Those who resented my leadership didn't last long with the Pals. The rest of the guys who stayed on realized that someone had to make the decisions and besides I was almost an adult. I took the bull by the horns and got things under way. I had the know-how of promoting, procuring, peddling, pleasing, and palavering with the people of the cities and towns that I visited in preparation for our coming event.

They were good times and bad times. We made friends easily, found property to perform at, visited a new town's newspapers first and the junkyards second. We squeezed by the insurance clauses, which was tough because the entire troupe, beyond myself, were minors. Our sponsors didn't know that, however, because the rest of the crew never showed up until the morning of the show.

W̲e played the second show of our career in our hometown of Pekin, and then set up to go to Champaign, Illinois, and got a good dose of experience, which is the best teacher, as I have learned.

You see, the town is the home of the University of Illinois. You better believe me when I tell you that when big schools are out for summer vacation, the last week of July is no time to draw spectators. You could shoot a cannon across Champaign-Urbana ten different ways without hitting a soul.

The absence was overwhelming and if I hadn't had the money from the "kitty," we would have never gotten to the next spot, Lincoln, Illinois, where we had a winner!

At Springfield, the fair was ready to blossom and I tried to get a chance to "bask"—play to the crowd and then take up a collection. I'd heard of it, but had never seen it done. We didn't earn much money that day for our pains, and I still haven't seen basking done.

Three weeks on the road, seven to ten people to feed and house, three dates. At the end of the summer, Satan's Pals arrived back in Pekin with exactly twice the money that we had started with.

A show was born.

Satan's Pals Ad. 1935
Newspaper advertisement for the third or fourth show performed by Satan's Pals—and the first show in our hometown of Pekin, Illinois. For this homecoming show, we pulled out all the stops and even drove a bicycle through a flaming board wall! I organized this ad with promotion for our various supporters, including Pekin Auto Body, with its ad line, "You Wreck 'em—We Fix 'em! Let Satan's Pals show you how cars are wrecked, let us show you how they're rebuilt."

35

CHAPTER 4

Make the Dash— and the Crash—With a Nash

Rollover, 1941
Material evidence of why we shied away from the wooden-frame cars. I performed this Rollover stunt at Steubenville, Ohio, in a 1923 steel-on-wood Chevrolet and was left sitting on the wooden frame holding the steering wheel. The steel body tore completely off the frame and kept on rolling down the infield.

Roll bars? Roll cages? Never heard of such contrivances.

The Lucky Lee Lott Hell Drivers trusted just three items for safety during a day of daredevilry: Lots of steel, lots of padding, and lots of skill.

In 1936, there was a meeting of the Lucky Lee Lott Hell Drivers President, Vice President, Manager, Engineer, Signwriter, Publicist, Equipment Overseer, Booking Agent, Advance Agent, Announcer, Wagonmaster, Personnel Director, and Key Performer at the office at 1211 Royal Avenue, Pekin, Illinois. The whole ball of wax was me, myself, and I. The members of the crew were out playing Kick the Can.

After the first year of Satan's Pals and now the Lucky Lee Lott Hell Drivers, I was convinced that there was one item on the agenda that topped all others in importance: Safety.

Safety meant skilled driving, well-planned stunts, and the right cars for the right show. I spent all my spare time during the winter at the dining room table with graph paper. This stunt with this much weight at that speed will give you this much lift, and so on. You had to get it on paper first.

But above all you had to have good machines.

How did we pick up the cudgel for any one car? Well, we learned the hard way early on just what cars to drive and how to prepare them.

I was a nineteen-year-old kid when I first placed the mantle of Hell Driver on my brand spanking new 1935 DeSoto Airflow and started my career as a car crasher. I had been high diver at the Chicago World's Fair and saved my pay to buy that DeSoto

Jumper Car, 1950
The trick was to pick the proper car for the proper stunt. If the car was going to leave the ground, you had to have anything but a wood-frame car. When Nash came out with its all-steel unit-bodied cars in 1949, the Hell Drivers immediately fell in love with them.

Nash Flyer, 1950
I always stood by Nash, and Nash always stood by me.

T-Bone Crash, 1939
Convertibles and cloth-roofed cars had their role in our stunts. At the Reading Fair in Pennsylvania, our clown took his girlfriend (a fellow Hell Driver in drag) for a ride—only to go off a ramp and leap through the air to t-bone another car. Upon impact, the clown went through the cloth roof and landed some feet down the track. After the smoke cleared, the "girlfriend," who had been belted into the back seat, casually opened the side door and asked the clown where he had gone to.

for $1,900. It was a good investment: I crashed through walls, did the high jumps, and everything in between with that Airflow—and it was still going strong when I retired it six years later in 1941.

My coterie of teenage daredevils and I used the cars as we found them when we were starting out, but our first performance as Satan's Pals taught us our first lesson. Lou "Batter" Crooks was doing our patented Glass Wall Crash on a motorcycle when a piece of the plate glass caught him in the leg. Thirty-three stitches later we swore off glass forever. From then on, the first thing we did in preparing our stunt cars was to take all of the prevailing glass windows out—except if we were going to do a Lake Jump and were in need of an oxygen supply while underwater.

We bought cars from boneyards, backlots, or dealerships in those days. Later on, we bought most of our stunt vehicles and

Brick Wall Crash, 1939
This stunt took a heavy toll on a car. With these early wood-framed vehicles, the frame would more than likely break in half upon impact. The driver rode in back with cushions and a wire to control the accelerator. This Auburn took the wall down at the old Candlestick Park in San Francisco.

catch cars from insurance or finance companies and made one car or motorcycle out of two. Or sometimes one out of three or four.

As I said, we began by junking the windows. Then we pulled off the bumpers, the spare seats, and any other parts that could possibly come loose in a crash. I learned early on that we had to clean up after ourselves when we performed. If we left hood ornaments and chromed trash scattered over a fair's racetrack, we wouldn't be playing those dates again in the future.

Next we tied down the hoods and trunks with straps so they wouldn't pop open during a crash or any other inopportune time. We always covered the batteries with a burlap pad to keep the acid from exploding or draining onto the track if the car rolled. Later, we replaced the wet cells with dry-cell lantern batteries and used our shoulders to give the cars a push to start. In addition, we often drained the radiator and cooling system for stunts as the cars would be in action for such a short period that they wouldn't overheat anyway. And we always kept the amount of gasoline in the car at a bare minimum, period. Didn't need to learn any lesson with that one. Figured it out in advance.

The trick was to pick the proper car for the proper stunt. If the car was going to leave the ground, you had to have anything but the 1914–1930 steel-on-wood vehicle. Many cars in those days had heavy steel bodies bolted to heavy wooden frames, and they were a sure recipe for disaster when they landed from a jump. The frame would more than likely break in half—usually with help from termites who had gotten a good head start before

War Bond Drive, 1943
Crashing cars to crash the Axis powers. Here we were doing our best to win the war by promoting war bond sales with a stunt show in downtown Lafayette Square in Buffalo, New York. "Over the top with the 5th war loan" was the message of the day. I bought this stunt car from the police impound lot and it arrived complete with a bullet hole in the cowling.

Proving Ground, 1952
Here the Hell Drivers donned their other outfits to test the rocker panel clearance on a prototype 1952 Golden Anniversary Nash designed by Pinin Farina. We did all sorts of crash tests, rollovers, and more, hiring ourselves out as "crash engineers"—or human crash test dummies, depending on your point of view. Our proving ground was located in Groveland, Illinois.

us—and the body would land in the dirt. Not very professional looking.

I avoided like the plague the weather-beaten steel-on-wood General Motors cars. They made good catch cars but little more.

Then came the introduction of the product called Plymouth. This primal product of basic no-wood-infested mobilization fit the bill for us for many a crash. The Plymouth was one piece of steel above the rockers and could endure just about anything we could dish out. The Plymouth did me well when I could lay my hands on the 1938–1939 models.

Ford? Well, Ford had done me well in the early days of Satan's Pals but they just weren't up to snuff for crashing. I did use them for years for precision driving, however.

Now, the Studebaker was always a car to be reckoned with, excepting for the deadly rust of doors and rockers. In 1946, I bought seventeen fleet cars of the Studebaker persuasion from an old taxicab builder in Peoria, Illinois. I trucked them up to Stude's South Bend factory, and then stripped them down to the frame and completely rebuilt the cars with parts from the works' "cull bins." After our rebuild work, we made twelve cars from those seventeen.

We were welcomed at the back door of Studebaker but never at the front. I had a going thing with the engineers at Stude but could never get the sales people together on a deal. Instead, we were granted entry at the back door and the privilege of scrounging parts from the scrap bins.

All things considered, there was one car that stood heads and tails above all the others: Nash.

Nash cars were always a delightful hunk of steel. I kept my eyes open for a Nash and paid a premium ($10) for a good-running Nash Lafayette, later built by Nash's subsidiary, Ajax. I could use those Nash-built cars for several stunts before giving them a siphon-hose resuscitation.

In 1948, I was engaged by Nash to run some diabolic proving ground tests. As a moonlighting job, the Hell Drivers did proving ground and testing work on contract, including crashing of experimental and prototype vehicles with ourselves serving double duty as living human crash test dummies. For Nash, the hot property was a prototype of its upcoming 1952 Nash model designed by Pinin Farina, marked as the firm's 50th Anniversary special.

Two of my top men were sent to handle the situation. As I told Lou Crooks, "Give it the best of the worst." I took off for Montana to book county fair dates and he took off for Nash HQ with a couple of trucks loaded with ramps and dynamite and all that good stuff.

Contract, 1949
This was my standard Hell Drivers contract through the 1950s. Motor Testing Engineers was my other moniker for the proving ground car-crash test work that we did for manufacturers such as Nash.

Greenhorn Nash Fleet, 1951
A fleet of thirty-eight Nashes on their way to becoming Hell Driver stunt cars. This was the day we took delivery of the new cars from a Detroit dealership. The cars were painted Pan American Red and would soon have the Lucky Lee Lott Hell Drivers name emblazoned across their sides with yellow and black paint.

Side-by-Side Jump, 1952

Our precision driving stunts included this four-car, one-ramp jump. Each Nash measured 16 inches from the inside of the tire to the outside of the chrome on the fenders—that's 32 inches of cars side by side on 28 inches of ramp. The driver who missed paid for the chrome. This was done at 50 mph, of course. Our drivers here were Max Schwab, Bob Beal, Eddie May, and Steve Stiles.

Nash Ads, 1950

Test drive a new Nash Airflyte yourself—but don't try these stunts at home!

It wasn't until several days later that I got a call at the lodge at Kalispell, Montana. It was Lou on the line and he was excited: "Boy, have I got the car for you." I had never heard Batter so worked up over a car. By the time he was done testing, he was sold. No matter how hard he tried, he couldn't kill that car.

I was on the prowl for the ideal stunt car, which I hoped to buy in lots of thirty at a time, each season replacing the fleet by disposing of the leftovers from the year before. With Batter's kind words for the Nash in mind, I sent out a prospectus to Nash asking for their backing in exchange for promoting their wares.

I was still out in Montana when I got word that a letter had come back to my Pekin office from Nash Motors' Sales Manager Stan Williamson saying he'd be happy to talk. The letter arrived on a Saturday; Monday morning I was waiting at his office door at Nash-Kelvinator, Plymouth Road, Detroit, Michigan.

Stan asked me how many cars I would need for the Hell Drivers.

I blue-skied it: "30," I told him, "and I want to buy them from you."

I wasn't asking for any handouts.

"Buy them?" Stan said, surprised. "What do you expect to pay for them?"

"Production cost," I replied.

"Well, that sounds OK, but I don't know what production cost is," he said. "Do you have any idea?"

I ran my gray matter's calculator fast. "In the neighborhood of

Three-Wheel Drive, 1952
By accident, I discovered that a 1952 Nash Statesman could be driven on city streets with only three wheels. A tight forward spin during a show tore the wheel off a car, but it was still driveable! Thus, we quickly developed it as part of our show by "prepping" cars to lose a wheel. Meanwhile, Nash advertised its cars around the country with the display pictured here.

$1,000 apiece," I guessed.

Stan signed on the dotted line.

Nash's Airflyte was the first mass-produced unit-body car, so it was ideal for our stuntwork. The car was streamlined and sharply styled—or a bathtub on wheels, depending on how you looked at it. It had a one-piece curved windshield and fully reclining front seats that converted into beds, perfect for our travelling. The car was years ahead of its time.

In our agreement, Nash Motors would boil-dip and magnaflux all of our cars at every stress point—all moving parts from connecting rods to draw bars, front wheel assemblies to tailpipes.

Tailpipes and mufflers?

Yep, that's the idea, those parts were stressed to the nth degree. When a car leaps into the air, airborne for 60 feet distance as high as 5 feet off the ground, the 60-pound muffler throws a leverage of three times its weight against the tailpipes, hangers, and frame mounts, so we had to be certain they were sturdy.

In the construction of the car for my use,

Nash Sales Show, 1952
Nash flyer to its dealers offering a Hell Drivers presentation at their dealerships to promote the cars. Who could resist a Nash after witnessing such stunts?

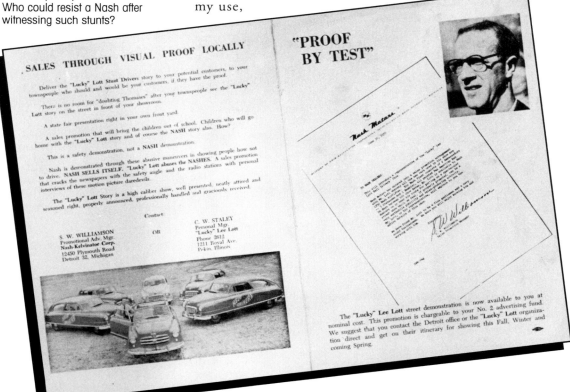

there were no variations from the cars delivered to the dealers for domestic sales. I did require heavy-duty Monroe shocks on all rolling stock, International 6.00x16 pickup wheels, and I made an essential requirement on the motor mounts. I used C-clip motor mounts rather than the biscuit types. We were changing too many of the factory-installed gadgets due to unusual torque of the motor due to the crash landings. As a result, standard Nash production picked up on our suggestion and converted to the C-type motor mount.

Each year after that, I would buy a fleet of new Nashes. One year, Nash was behind schedule, so it shipped us four black-and-white police cars that were supposed to go to Des Moines.

That first year, 1949, all of my Nash Airflytes were painted Pan American Red. In later years, we used different Nash models painted in different colors.

When we'd take delivery on the cars from Nash, we'd take the 6.00x15 wheels and tires off the cars and place International pickup Kelsey-Hayes 6.00x16 wheels and tires on the equipment, leaving the take-offs in winter quarters for the season. We'd then cover the upholstery with slip-on covers, remove the floor and trunk mats, cover the armrests on the driver's side, and take off the front door thresholds—anything that would show wear. We put the Hell Drivers lettering on the cars with sign-painter's enamel.

At the end of the season, we used Red Devil Paint Remover and wiped the lettering away. I then resold the cars at a dealers' auction in "as is" condition as "show cars"—but didn't specify what kind of show.

I stuck by Nash from 1949 through to 1955, and I put a lot of faith in those cars. Our first Nash was used for 126 leaps of 50–75 feet distance as high as 14 feet into the air straight up. By rights that car should have had square wheels. At the end of the season it was sold and was still roaming the streets of my old hometown as late as 1970.

In the end, I put 382 Nash cars out to pasture.

A Hell Drivers show had many backbones. The announcer, the clowns, the daredevils, the bill posters, the mechanics, and good cars. Any shortcomings and I took the blame. The credits went to the products and performers.

Nash News, 1951
Nash promoted racing, records, and stunts performed with its cars. Alongside NASCAR and speed records, here were the Hell Drivers testing Nashes "by torture."

Human Battering Ram, 1940

Ah, there was nothing like the battering ram! We had several styles in which we performed this stunt: This was the best—and most dangerous. Here Joe Rodman was strapped to the front of our stunt car with a pillow behind his back and a motorcycle helmet pointed to the front....

Human Battering Ram, 1940

...And here he comes through the flaming board wall, a human cow catcher at York, Pennsylvania. Joe made the mistake of forgetting to put the metal guards inside his boots to protect his shins while doing this stunt. He only made that mistake once!

CHAPTER **5**

Birth of the Hell Drivers— and Famous Last Words

F amous last words: "I'll never head-on another two-door."
Those words were muttered by Hell Driver Bob Kill in 1939 as the Lucky Lee Lott Hell Drivers performed their world tour of Michigan.

The Ingham County Fair in Mason, Michigan, to be more exact. This was the scene of Bob Kill trying to get the cushion hinge off the back of the front seat of a two-door Chevrolet and put it into his pocket at 60 mph before hitting me in a four-door Pontiac head-on.

Let me re-route that with an explanation.

I n 1939, we were a bunch of greenhorns still wet behind the ears. Satan's Pals had given way to the Lucky Lee Lott Hell Drivers way back in October 1935. We were now a professional daredevil gang, but we were still learning our lessons by the black and blue and the bumps and scrapes as long as God was on our side and we had enough money for gasoline and bologna.

Our Michigan world tour for 1939 took us through dates at Adrian and Marshall, then Grayling, Coldwater, Charlotte, and Kalamazoo. We played Jackson to fill in for another show called the Legion of Daredevils, which had had its motorcycles repossessed and its daredevil locked up by the sheriff before the show could begin, and then went to Kalamazoo, where the grandstand roof was blown away by a tornado just days before we were due.

And then there was the Ingham County Fair in Mason.

Our feature of the day when solid junkers were available was The Head-On Collision of two cars with the drivers remaining in the cars' back seats. We also did our usual Board Wall Crashes,

Bob Kill
Famous last words: "I'll never head-on another two-door." He did survive, however. He was primarily a motorcycle stuntman and actually took many harder knocks on the cycles. Here he is in 1990 with one of my restored Hell Driver cars.

Bus Jump, 1946
High in the sky with a Hell Drivers Studebaker stunt car over a city bus and a stake bed truck at Logansport, Indiana. The 1933 Studebaker Rockne's wheels became square after 125 of these jumps.

Ski Jump, 1941
Diversify meant to add new stunts, so here we created The Ski Jump by jumping a 1926 Chevrolet four-door off a ramp and through a board wall at Stratford, Ontario.

Human Battering Ram, Human Jack, Rollover, and various and sundry offerings that would make the hairs stand on end just as high as that tornado in Kalamazoo. In fact, our T-Bone Crash had a strong effect on the teenagers of Michigan; when one Hell Driver was transported to the waiting ambulance for his efforts only to bounce off the stretcher before it got to the meat wagon, one teenage spectator wasn't able to hold his excitement and let it run down the legs of his trousers.

For the finale of the Hell Drivers show that day, we had two good junkers for The Head-On. Problem was, one junker was only a two-door. See, for The Head-On, the Hell Drivers got their respective cars motivating and aimed, then dove into the back seat with lots of padding and a wire to run the throttle. Now, we had a solid 1926 Pontiac four-door that was a wooden-bodied, good-running bucket of bolts with a solid front seat. Fine. But the only other junker we could come by was a 1929 Chevrolet two-door with a foldable forward front seat used to let the back seat passengers in and out.

There was no solution to the dilemma so Bob Kill and yours truly drew straws as to who would get the four-door and who would suffer the two-door. We couldn't flip coins because we didn't have them, hadn't gotten our part of the take from the fair board yet.

Anyway, Lucky's luck held out and Bob Kill got the short end.

It was a fine Sunday afternoon. Our show had been going great guns and was up to the finale. We had a good crowd, the best for the weeks

Poster, 1935
"Held Over"—an early poster for the Hell Drivers in our first year on the round. Satan's Pals became the Lucky Lee Lott Hell Drivers in October 1935.

Logo Plan, 1936
My original drawings for the Lucky Lee Lott Hell Drivers logo as used from October 1935 through 1955.

Board Wall Plans, 1935

My original plans for the board wall used for The Human Battering Ram and numerous other stunts. For stunts where we lit the wall on fire, I noted "Don't use over 1 qt. gasoline." Smart words.

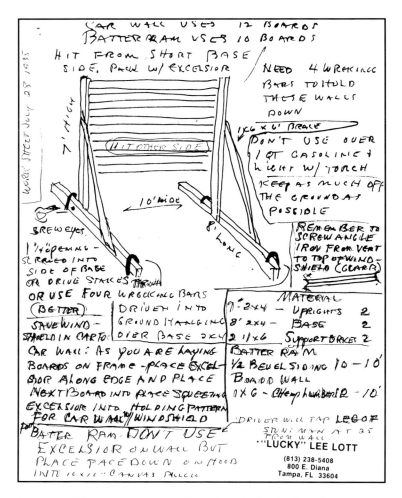

just past. The popcorn was all sold and the junkyard men were ready to pick up the junkers we'd rented. Except for the last two, the aforementioned Chevrolet and Pontiac.

The Head-On finale was announced by Billy Newell and our cars came barrelling down the track. I was headed left and Bob Kill was headed right coming up the track for the home stretch where we would crash directly in front of the grandstand for all of the world—or at least all of the denizens of Ingham County Michigan—to witness. Coming out of the right curve, it was difficult to pick up speed and control the steering of the junker, so we both had our hands full driving those cars like Roman charioteers steering with one hand and pulling the accelerator with the wire.

With our aim settled, I ducked behind the back seat, held onto the accelerator wire, and wished Bob well.

Dive Bomber, 1950

The Dive Bomber stunt was a combination of our great T-Bone Crash and a flying start from a ramp. Gravity helped magnify the resulting collision to great effect. Here, I was at the wheel of the flying 1928 Essex landing on the 1927 Oldsmobile at Sioux Falls, South Dakota.

Dive Bomber, 1940

In retrospect, the Dive Bomber stunt may have been better named The Kamikaze. Here's Hell Driver "Coach" Vic Caldwell of Concord, North Carolina, coming in for a hard landing and t-boning the crash car, which rolled with the blow.

Brick Wall Crash, 1939
This stunt worked just as its name described: Set up a wall of bricks (without mortar) and run a car into it. Here's the moment of impact at York, Pennsylvania....

Crew Chiefs, 1946
Hell Driver crew chiefs for each of my four outfits that were simultaneously touring different parts of the United States. From left, Phil Rakestraw of Manito, Illinois; Joe Lange of Noware, Kentucky; Nifty Fargo of Vero Beach, Florida; and Louis "Batter" Crooks of Pekin.

Brick Wall Crash, 1939
...And here's the results when the smoke and dust have cleared. The trick behind the stunt was to brace yourself well for the crash. That's Fargo walking toward the results; he had planned on going fishing with the owner of that 1929 Nash. Boy, those old Nashes were tough cars!

Buckle Up For Safety:
Fitting Safety Harnesses to Hell Driver Cars

Seatbelts were unheard of by the normal joe in the days when the Lucky Lee Lott Hell Drivers began their shows. Seatbelts were not available on most of your typical road-going passenger cars through even the 1950s. But when doing a Head-On Crash or a Bus Jump they were a necessity.

A daredevil's safety harness is a far cry from the average seatbelt, however.

In fitting a car for a safety harness, we would start with a 10-pound bar with a pointed end and poke a hole through the floorboards on both sides of the driver's seat. Through the holes we ran links of heavy-duty steel chain, which was fastened to the frame of the stunt car.

The chain was then connected to army air force surplus training plane harnesses. Problem was, those airplane harnesses were made out of canvas webbing and the stuff wore out, so we converted them by adding horsehide belts that could stand up to any punishment.

The safety belt used by the professional Hell Driver holds the daredevil in place with a leather belt that measures 4 inches wide and 3/16 inches thick. The belt runs across the driver's lap and into the proverbial "crack" where the edge of the seat and the back of the seat joins.

The posturing of the belt in this manner permits the driver to lay over on his right side and brace the upper part of the body with his left arm against the solid part of the dashboard of the car.

Poster, 1935
"2 Hour Circus of Death."

Head-On Crash, 1938
In the early days, we did The Head-On while riding on the car's running boards, crashing, and then flying with the momentum.
Later on, we rode the crash out from the back seat. Except for the time, that is, when Bob Kill got the short straw and did The Head-On in a two-door car with foldable front seats.

Now, we had reinforced Bob's foldable split front seat cushion with a couple 2x4s but we weren't expecting miracles from pine boards. The windshields and all the glass were removed from both cars as always so no one would get hit by flying glass. Bob hid behind his seat and braced himself for the crash.

We met at about 50 mph apiece—100 mph aggregate speed—having laid over sideways against the cushion with our backs against said cushion and letting go of the wire controlling the speed. We laid down that way when we were about 30 feet apart and pointed the cars to meet with the right front frame horn of each car aimed into the center of the radiator of the other car.

The crash was everything you would expect—and more. There was torn metal, there was smoke, there was noise.

And Bob Kill took a spill.

My four-door served me according to Hoyle's. My solid front seat broke, absorbing the shock. But Bob's front seat swung forward with the impact, breaking the 2x4s, and he went over the top.

When the smoke had cleared. I climbed off the back floor and what did I see? There, lodged in the two-door's front windshield opening, was Bob Kill's rear end viewed from the back. The rear seat cushion had acted as a projectile and boosted Bob right into the windshield opening backwards.

It took some effort to get Bob loose but he wasn't hurt. All shook up, would describe his state of mind.

As we shook hands and took the plaudits of the grandstand, Bob muttered those famous last words to me, "I'll never head-on another two-door."

We cleaned up the track and got our share of the gate receipts.

I never did like a two-door car.

CHAPTER 6

A Day in the Daredevil's Life

Poster, 1947
"Motion picture daredevils in action!" This show drew the largest daredevil crowd in the Indian a State Fair's history.

My life has been one of many close shaves—and I don't mean in the barber's chair either. When things go right in the production of a motorized thrill show, all is well and good. When things go wrong, they really go wrong. When that happens, look out for St. Peter. Please take my hand.

So it was August 24, 1952.

"You can't afford to miss it. Get your tickets now. The world's safest drivers in the world's wildest show will roar into action in just fifteen minutes," said the voice over the loudspeaker at the DuQuoin State Fair in Illinois.

"You've seen these daredevil drivers in *Life*, *Pick*, *Parade*, and *Click* magazines. Now is your opportunity to see them in person on the racetrack of the DuQuoin State Fair, right here, this afternoon. The Lucky Lee Lott Hell Drivers. Rolling cars over and over, smashing autos into solid brick walls, crashing through walls of fire. You'll see new Nash Airflyte automobiles driven around the track on two wheels. You'll see these brand-new Nash Airflytes leaping high into the air over unbelievable hurtles. You're going to see the world-famous Illinois native son leap a car into the forty-feet deep lake on the infield at 60 miles per hour. Lucky Lee Lott will remain in the car and does not have diving equipment.

"All this and more. Get your tickets now!"

So it was with the barker at the grandstand ticket office. The loudspeakers blared in such a volume that would soon drive everyone to the grandstand if only to get away from the noise.

"Come on Hank," a midway patron called back to his buddy. "I don't want to miss this."

Human Battering Ram, 1939
Hell Driver Al Perry rides the hood through a blazing one-inch thick board wall with yours truly at the wheel performing at Soldier Field, Chicago.

"Aw, hell. Let's not get sucked in on that deal. It's just another gimmick to get our money. They don't do nothing we ain't seen before. Those jerks get cars given to them by the car companies and try to see how much they can mess them up—and they get paid for trying! They act nervous and all and jolt a few swigs to get goin' and we're supposed to pay to see 'em?" argued his friend.

"You know what I read in Sunday's *Springfield State Journal?*" queried the other. "This guy Lucky Lee Lott, from up Pekin way, is supposed to jump a car off a high ramp into the lake that was cut out of this land when there used to be a coal mine here. That's what was here when they built the fair. That lake is 100 feet deep. I don't want to miss it!"

"Aw, shoot. The guy on the loudspeaker said the lake was only 40 feet deep."

"Yea, but it would be a good trick even if he didn't make it. As long as he stays in the car. He will won't he?"

"What's the ding?"

"A whole buck."

"Do you think he'll stay in the car?"

"The newspaper said he stayed in the car under water 12 minutes one time."

"He's probably got an air tank with him."

"Let's go, we'd spend that much on the kewpie doll joint anyway."

That afternoon was one of the prettiest that God ever put down on Earth. The sun was shining. The temperature was about 80 degrees. A nice breath of breeze blew across the grandstand, coming into the infield from the lake, just enough to help keep the spectators comfortable. The "butchers" were selling trinkets, novelties, ice cream, soda pop, and everything else to get the money. The show clowns were teasing the kids and the girls, chasing each other around, known as "working the come-in." Stragglers were still trying to find a spare seat. The grandstand was filling with 15,000 people.

At 2:25, "Toad" Corriel, my clown, took center stage and mike and went into a lip-sync of Victor Borge's "Phonetic Punctuation." Toad had made an on-the-air recording at a Borge concert one time and did a remarkable act with it. He got a great hand, went into a Sousa number, and followed immediately with the theme music of the Hell Drivers show called "Comedian's Gallop." Adrenalin was flowing. The crowd was ready for action.

At 2:30, Don Kelso, the Lucky Lee Lott Hell Drivers announcer and emcee, took the track mike, acknowledged the sponsors: Nash Motors, the Goodyear Tire and Rubber Company, the Quaker State Oil Company, Standard Oil of Indiana, and the local Nash dealer, who furnished the fifteen junkers that were to be smashed in the afternoon show.

Kelso gave the spectators a few points of interest about the daredevil business: You don't take a chance unless you have one. A daredevil does nothing for nothing, he gets paid for what he does. If others try the sort of thing you see done here, you'll pay the difference between a daredevil and a darn fool. The darn fool tries the stunt and then thinks about it afterwards—if he is able. The daredevil thinks a stunt out and then does it.

Zam! Pow! Bang! And all hell broke loose.

Roaring engines from both ends of the track!

Daredevil drivers from all directions driving brand-new ivory-colored Italian Pinin Farina-styled Nash Airflytes with black tops and the bright yellow Lucky Lee Lott Hell Drivers moniker emblazoned on the sides came roaring down the racetrack at a given signal. Each driver was introduced.

Kelso roared over the mike, "One of the original Lucky Lee Lott Hell Drivers, originating in Pekin, Illinois. Here is Lou 'Batter' Crooks."

Batter spun in sideways and received heavy applause.

Car number 2 from the other end of the track.

"From Hollywood, California, Jack Cavalli."

Car number 3 slid into position in front of the crowd.

"From Odessa, Texas, Jimmie Cook!"

Car number 4 up next.

"From Toledo, Ohio, Phil Rakestraw."

Car number 5 roared down the stretch to do his side spin and disgorge the driver.

"From Helsinki, Finland, and Helsinki, Michigan, here is the Fearless Finn, Hank Hackili.

"And the man you've been waiting for! From Pekin, Illinois, the home of another well-known and famous person, Everett Dirksen. Now wait, this is not Everett Dirksen in this car—it's Lucky Lee Lott, whose name you see on the sides of the cars!"

Poster, 1942
"See Superman leap his car over a transcontinental bus!" and "Smashing jalopies to smash the Japs." Those were the days!

Car number 6 comes on in reverse, doing a 180-degree spin to stop with the car facing the grandstand. I jumped out, taking the applause of those 15,000 plus people and setting that crowd into one screaming wave of humanity. The crowd went absolutely wild, like they had no idea that I was going to appear here, believing they were going to be fed a piece of the show while the "name" was somewhere else. Some were probably expecting the Tournament of Spills or whatever dinky shows had been seen around the state. The billing, however, had stated that Lucky Lee Lott would be there in person and it took five minutes for the spectators to take their seats again.

The show started with a warm-up run and a couple of opening stunts like The Slide for Life, The Human Battering Ram, and high-side driving with the new Nash Airflytes on two wheels as advertised. With some four and six precision driving cars side by side and single-file fashion and the overtures done, next up was stunt number 8 on the program.

Kelso again, "What would happen if a husband would lie on the grass in the backyard and say, 'Would you please drive the car over me honey?'

Human Jack, 1949

Vic Caldwell's first try at the Human Jack stunt while in Lubbock, Texas. Harley Cook was at the wheel with Lucky Lee Lott instructing on the finer points. The board was securely staked down at one end, and the car travelled at no more than 12 1/2 mph. A simple stunt that was not dangerous in the least.

Human Jack, 1952

Sixteen-year-old Bob Reiling as the Human Jack (with his parent's consent). Nash requested that we rename our show the Stunt Stars as painted on this 1952 Nash stunt car. After two shows of empty grandstands, we repainted the cars with our tried-and-true Hell Drivers' moniker.

"Just don't even think of it. Just watch now as our daredevils will provide the know-how of this particular stunt. It is not as easy as it looks here. And incidentally, you of the younger generation, the things you're seeing done here this afternoon are done by professionals and are not for the street, highway, or backroad by crazies. These men are schooled and trained in these stunts, this occupation. These daredevils would not go into a doctor's, dentist's, or any other professional room and try the things they do there; those professionals would not try this particular type of vocational activity. End of sermon!

"I see the men have the next act ready and we can get on with the act called The Iron Man, or also known as The Human Jack as the program says. It all started over at the town called St. Louis, with Iron Man Al Perry in 1926 and performed at that time with the popular automobile called the Overland. Al Perry would travel the carnival circuits, promoting the Overland dealers to bring a car out to the carnival grounds and let his son drive the car over his body.

"Nothing much at all has changed since that time except there's a slight difference in the looks of the cars. Our daredevil performing this stunt today is the youngest performer with the Lucky Lee Lott Hell Drivers. He does not use a gimmick, prop, or doohickey to take the weight of the car. He will perform in a pair of bathing trunks so that everyone can see that he doesn't have a steel corset around his midriff. The plank is 5 feet long, 2 inches thick, and 18 inches wide, staked securely to the ground with a pair of axle rods as you can see the men preparing for the stunt now."

"Here he is from Manito, Illinois, sixteen-year-old Bob Reiling."

He was given a strong ovation and many cheers and signs from the bobby-soxers for Bob was picked for this particular stunt for musculature. Bob assumed his position on the track beneath the far end of the board so that it was resting on that portion of his body between his knee caps and his floating ribs, directly over his pelvis.

The unit manager, Nifty Fargo of Vero Beach, Florida, aimed the car directly at the board so that the left wheels of the car would hit dead center. This accomplished, Fargo completed the run at 12 1/2 mph and Bob leapt to his feet and took the plaudits of the crowd.

"Event number 23 coming up. A crew of Lucky Lee Lott men are over on the infield preparing for the next event of the afternoon program. You've no doubt heard from advance publicity that Lucky Lee Lott will attempt one of his motion picture stunts of leaping a car into a lake. The fact that the DuQuoin Fairgrounds

---

The difference between a daredevil and a darn fool is that the darn fool tries the stunt and then thinks about it afterwards—if he is able. The daredevil thinks a stunt out and then does it.

The Big Jump, 1951

A Hell Driver goes for distance at Peoria, Illinois, over our car transporter and a lineup of catch cars, and landed 142 feet down the track. The goal was to land on the catch cars but this driver—who will remain unidentified—chose to go for speed and distance. He did the infamous pancake landing on the flat and learned his lesson well. We typically used up eight to ten catch cars and junkers per show.

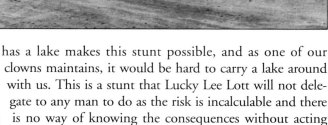

Program, 1942

We played the New York Polo Grounds as part of the Wild West Rodeo, which intermixed bare-back bronc riding, Captain Bill Baker diving 90 feet into a pool of flaming oil, bears riding motorcycles, knife-throwing acts, and our patented Dive Bomber crash. Now that was a show!

has a lake makes this stunt possible, and as one of our clowns maintains, it would be hard to carry a lake around with us. This is a stunt that Lucky Lee Lott will not delegate to any man to do as the risk is incalculable and there is no way of knowing the consequences without acting them out himself."

Kelso continued his description, "Lucky Lee Lott has gained his reputation throughout the past eighteen years by originating and performing new stunts, and will not—and has not—let anyone do a stunt that he has not done himself and mastered.

"At this time, if you will cast your eyes to the right center of the infield on the opposite shore you will see an automobile painted silver so that it will be visible at the bottom of the lake. This car will be used in the thrilling Lake Jump.

"You'll also see a set of ramps out there set up about 40 feet from the edge of the lake. These ramps are 4 feet high and 28 feet long. Lucky will take his car around the perimeter of the infield, cut sharply at the proper time and head into line with the ramps. His speed at takeoff should be 57 miles per hour. He will leap the car upward about 20 feet and out over the lake about 110 feet—out to the deepest part of the lake. Lucky will of course be wearing a daredevil's life insurance, his safety belt, the same safety belt used in the World War II P-38 Lightning fighter aircraft.

"Now we see Lucky Lee Lott is ready for the one-way boat ride. May we present again the master of the thrill show world, Lucky Lee Lott of Pekin, Illinois."

"It was the wildest ovation I've ever experienced since the grandstand was built a few years ago," said Mr. W. R. Hayes, President of the DuQuoin State Fair. Mr. Hayes passed away a week after the fair that year, following his dream of a fair of this magnitude for southern Illinois.

Lou "Batter" Crooks was already in the rowboat that was to take me to the island as opposed to driving all the way around to the back and crossing the bridge in the back near the barns. I got into the boat, with him at the oars. He was shaking so badly that I had to help him put the oar locks into the holes. I had to reach forward and give him a hand and I said, "Hey, what are you so nervous about? I'm the one that's going to do the jump." He hadn't been with me on any previous Lake or River Jumps. He had been in the service in Germany and Japan when I started the water jumps and was late in getting back into the swing of things.

"You're still going through with it?" asked Batter, as if he had to.

I threw my hiking thumb across the lake pointing to the grandstand and said, "When a stunt has been announced, it's going to be performed. You know that."

"I'm not an eager beaver, but if you're leg won't take it, I'd like to try." Batter offered.

I had had the misfortune of tearing a tendon in a highway accident when I took to the ditch to avoid a collision with a cow on a Minnesota county fair date run three weeks before the DuQuoin fair. I got out of the cast five days before this date. It had never bothered my performances once the cast had dried.

"No, but thanks Batter. You take the next Lake Jump. We've got one coming up in Ohio in September." (He did get that chance and Batter did a perfect jump. It was a beaut, I might say.)

As we rowed across the lake toward the car, the spectators were quieter than anything I ever experienced. Usually they're like the Spanish crowds roaring to have the bulls come out of the chute. Noise and din and all that stuff, but now it was really quiet. Even the candy butchers were silent, and that's something.

Batter had been with the show before the war and he was aware of what crowd reactions used to be like.

"They're waiting for the kill," Batter opened, "and don't give them the satisfaction. Just make it your usual perfection."

My retort was, "I'll do my best to please and disappoint them at the same time."

Batter grounded the skiff and we walked up to the prearranged car. The belt was in place. All the glass was left in the car contrary to our on-land stunts; the windows were rolled shut. The bumpers

The slamming of the door made it a small world. The door shut out the rest of the universe, the cares and worries and stuff that one thinks about beforehand.

Slide for Life, 1949
First, you get a cowhide apron to sit on, strap yourself to the back of a stunt car, and then hold on tight as you slide through a flaming field of gasoline. This was Jim Wadsworth's first try at the stunt, at Lubbock, Texas.

were left on for this stunt as it makes it easier to grab hook the sunken car if necessary. The doors were not locked nor wired shut. I got behind the wheel and snapped the belt in place and turned on the key. It was a go as I revved it up to a couple of thousand rpm and was ready to slip my helmet on my head.

"Are you going to wear your glasses?" Batter asked.

"I really don't need them. I've got the road map in my mind. Here take them. I'll make it OK." Then I thought, those glasses might be my good luck charm—if I believed in such stuff.

As long as I've known Batter Crooks—and that's all his life— I've never seen such a worried look in his eyes. He was a pal when

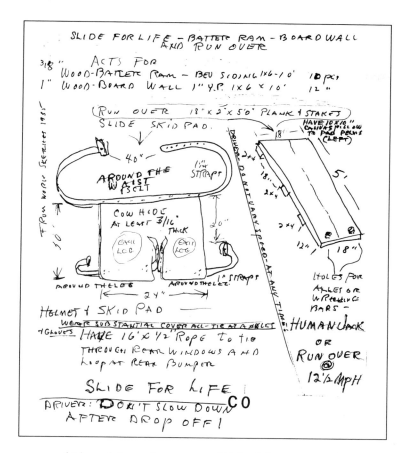

Slide for Life Plans, 1935
My original plans for the cowhide apron required to do The Slide for Life. My note to the driver was especially pertinent with this stunt: "Don't slow down after drop off!" When the stuntman let go from the car, he would keep on sliding for a short distance and we didn't want him to rear-end the stopped vehicle.

we were kids and through our teens. He had the scariest, downright forlorn aspect as he tapped my shoulder before I rolled the window shut and he had said good luck and crossed his fingers as he had a habit of doing before and during a rough one.

The slamming of the door made it a small world. This was it. The door shut out the rest of the universe, the cares and worries and stuff that one thinks about beforehand. The world had become a 100-cubic-foot steel and glass atrium. I checked the bind on my belt, snapped the chin strap on my helmet, spit on my roping gloves that I always wear. And I too crossed my fingers with a quick prayer.

I revved the engine again and sounded the OK. I swung around to start across the field to line up. Backed up a bit to a distance of about an eighth of a mile and took aim.

The grooms and stable boys had left some horses to graze on the infield bluegrass. These beautiful beasts looked up when they heard the roaring thunder of the racing automobile that had invad-

The Lake Jump, 1952

I knew I was going too fast the moment I left the ramp at DuQuoin. The car hit the water with a slap and then quickly sank to the bottom 40 feet below. We settled upside down into three feet of mud and silt. I say we and I mean the car, myself, and God.

The Lake Jump, 1952

This was almost my last stunt ever. Four and a half minutes after sinking to the bottom, I emerged with thanks to Heavens and a full-throated Rebel Yell.

ed their sanctuary and so scampered away to find a quieter spot upon which to graze.

I adjusted my aim on the center of the ramps, and sped across the sod, watching for the track that my crew had made when they laid the potential course I was to take. The smoothest possible. Even so, there were some dips that made it debatable that I had the best course. But as I was closing in on the ramps there was a point of no return and I wasn't going to turn it off if I could help it. This was not one of those blood pumpers, this was the real thing. I wasn't in the mood for anything but to get the job done right then.

But then, between the time the ramps were set the night before and here at show time, gophers or some such little beasts had dug a hole right in the path of my takeoff. I should have left my glasses on my head. I did cut it short without knocking down the ramps and returned to the starting point. In the meantime, Batter had taken a shovel and filled the hole and packed it and then gave me the signal to try again. This time I picked my way a little more carefully and was able to find a course that was just about as smooth as the time they hauled me out of the operating room from the tendon operation in Minnesota.

The ramps were coming up at me with increasing speed, getting higher and longer all the time. As I hit the approach boards, I suddenly realized that I was traveling entirely too fast. I had planned upon hitting at about 45 mph and here I was airborne at 67 mph. It was difficult to gauge on the infield as opposed to the racetrack.

The car roared up and away. The grandstand to my right disappeared from sight and I got that feeling. The nose of the car started to drop and dropped too fast. I was some 20 feet off the water and turning over endways. I knew I was in for a loop. I had done one like this at another time, but that one was on the ground. Here came the full impact on the windshield.

Twenty-eight hundred pounds of steel smacking against the lake full of water—something had to give, and did. The windshield imploded on me. The force of the water cleared any fogginess that might have invaded my head and I was wide awake and started to battle for my life. The car rapidly sank to the bottom. I felt where the windshield had been and there was nothing but mud.

We were upside down and settling into 3 feet of silt at the bottom of 40 feet of water. We. Yes, I said we. God, the car, and I were in this mess together. So I said, Dear God, let's get out of here. And God, please take me with you, one way or the other.

I stopped worrying and started to think. I unsnapped the seat-

> We were upside down and settling into 3 feet of silt at the bottom of 40 feet of water. We. Yes, I said we. God, the car, and I were in this mess together.

belt. Next I rolled open a window. In came mud. I went to another window, rolled it open: mud. At about this time, the water started to clear and I saw a light brown streak of light coming from above me. This was no time for a panic. About four minutes without air. I shoved a cushion away that had been left in the car. I knew I couldn't break the back window glass with my hands, so I stood on my hands and kicked out the back glass with my feet, pulled away some shards that plummeted through the broken window and made a quick splash for daylight, 40 feet straight up.

Timed from the moment that the car left the ramp to when I surfaced it was exactly four and one half minutes without air. Since that time I've carried oxygen, but never needed it.

As my emcee Don Kelso remembered, "The 15,000 people in the grandstand didn't believe what they had seen. About half of the Lucky Lee Lott team were down to no shoes, no shirts, and almost no anything. Batter dove into the water, pushing the skiff the direction in which he had seen the Boss go under. On this side, Phil, Eddie, Henry, Joe, Dennis—everyone who could swim—were ready to go in when all of a sudden Lucky's head broke the surface.

"No one said a word until Lucky Lee Lott let out what might be called a 'Rebel Yell.'"

Batter Crooks continued, "As I had stepped back to take a running dive to where the skiff had drifted, I was peeled to my skivvies and was in the water when Lucky's head came to the surface. I pushed the boat so he'd have something to grab hold of because I knew that he just about had it. I boosted him into the boat and started to paddle to shore.

"From the time Lee's car disappeared in the water until his head came to the surface, you could hear a pin drop in that grandstand of 15,000 people. No one made a sound. Not even the candy butchers. It was totally unreal. But when his head came up and hit the surface of the lake, the top of the grandstand just about blew off." His words verbatim.

And Kelso remembered, "I was in London on VE Day and it was nothing like the noise emanating from the grandstand that afternoon welcoming Lucky Lee Lott's escape from what they thought was his last stunt. The people of southern Illinois really had their teeth shaken that afternoon. They were ready to go home after that. They thought that the show was over with. But The Lake Jump was an anti-climax."

Don Kelso leaped to the microphone and advised the public, "Just hold on for a few minutes until Lucky gets into dry clothes. Just settle down and we'll take a short intermission. Let the vendors serve you, and you folks sit back for a rest after that action. What did we tell you? Didn't we say you'd see action here this afternoon?"

Three or four minutes later I reappeared, dry and fresh, to a thunderous acclaim and came to the mike for a talk on careful driving on the highway.

The remainder of the show featured a car jumping over an auto transporter by Jack Cavalli. For the grand finale, another car was blown up with 10 pounds of dynamite with Steve Stiles at the wheel.

Just another day in the daredevil's life.

World Record Leap, 1942

Perhaps my greatest stunt of all time, holder of the world record for automobile leaps: 169 feet distance while travelling 35 feet vertically. I probably could have gone for more distance if the darn suicide door on my car hadn't flown open. This record jump was performed at Steubenville, Ohio.

World Record Leap, 1942

Another view of my great leap, which not only covered record distance but jumped over a school bus and several crash cars. This was also the sole stunt where I was seriously injured: I broke my back back upon landing. The resulting crick in my back unfortunately kept me out of the armed services in World War II. The further you leap, the easier you land—if, that is, you keep the rear wheels of the car 8 inches lower than the front upon landing.

The Invisible Jump

The Big Jump was big in more ways than one. It was big in terms of distance and it was big in terms of the crash landing at the end.

Thus, it was only right that The Big Jump be the finale of a Hell Driver show.

Now, doing The Big Jump was probably our most difficult—or at least, most dangerous—stunt. With all its attendant risks, The Big Jump was usually reserved for myself or one of the most senior, experienced, or talented of Hell Driver daredevils.

Consider the facts. The Hell Driver circled the racetrack twice to get his car up to speed, then aimed said vehicle at the high ramp, and took off on wings and a prayer, sailing over a school bus and landing smack dab on a batch of crash cars at the far end of the bus. This was accompanied by more than a stunt's fair share of drama, followed by lots of torn metal, smoke, dust, and noise, finished up with a hushed crowd waiting to see the Hell Driver pound open the jumper car's door and emerge safe and sound to their cheers.

And then there was the time I performed The Invisible Jump.

The beautiful scenery on a glowing summer afternoon up in the Poconos is the kind of sight that made the life of the itinerant showman all the more pleasurable. The Poconos blossom just where the western tip of New Jersey nestles into the northeastern tip of Pennsylvania—Wayne County, Pennsylvania, to be more explicit. It was 1939, and we were scheduled to play the Wayne County Fair at Honesdale, Pennsylvania. The village of about 5,000 people at that time had a fine fairground surrounded by gorgeous scenery and it was a joy to perform for the crowd.

Crash Landing, 1945
We threw out all of the stops for this show at New Ulm, Minnesota, on VJ Day! Jimmie Cook did The Big Jump—and added a Dive Bomber t-bone crash as a finale.

The Big Jump was big in more ways than one. It was big in terms of distance and it was big in terms of the crash landing at the end.

Never Underestimate the Job of a Clown

Would you consider doing anything for a laugh?

Well, the business of clowning generally means that person placing himself in a position of ridicule—but never one of sheer stupidity. He puts the impression across that he is stupid, but you'd better not let a good working clown hear you call him stupid.

The clowns with the Lucky Lee Lott Hell Drivers were far from stupid when it came to performing with the cars on the track. The clowns themselves were just as able and capable at stunting as the majority of the drivers.

There is a law of singular domain, which means two bodies cannot occupy the same space at the same time. For example, if a car and a clown are on the same ramp, the clown can quickly give up his occupancy to that spot when the car is on the other end of the ramp approaching at 55 mph. If he doesn't, something has got to give.

A working clown, by desire of survival, must wear gym or tennis shoes, but most do not lace them all the way up. I learned this lesson the hard way.

For instance, years ago, while playing the role of "come in" clown, Humphrey Q. Shagnausty (that was me in disguise for the day) was getting the crowd's adrenalin flowing while the latecomers were getting into their seats. We had the cars barking on the racetrack, making noises like the show was ready to start. The ramps were set for approach from either direction, so Hump was out there directing traffic. The two drivers on the track were novice rookies and got to practice this way before the show. I motioned for them to do a Head-On Crossover and I was to stand between the two cars, a 28 inch ramp sloping both ways, 24 inches high at the top. I was in the middle of the ramp while the two cars, with a combined tread width of 38 inches, were going to pass with me standing there. I did a duck stance, with my feet pointed in opposite directions up and down the ramp. They were supposed to ride the outside edge with their left tires.

One driver, I won't say who, took his 6 inches out of the center of the ramp—and the heel of my sneaker along with it. Wow! I had a Stop sign and a Go sign in each hand but I still don't know what happened to them 'cause I went straight up in the air—by this time the cars were clear of the ramps—and did a back flip to safety.

I did lose the back of my sneaker and had a sunburned heel for a week.

For the Lucky Lee Lott Hell Drivers, we had white-face clowns, jugglers, daredevil clowns, and all sorts of combinations thereof.

Don Adams—alphabetically first—was a bicycle clown. He did a breakaway series of tricks with his two-wheel bike, cannibalized it, and rode the last wheel off the stage without a bike. Don did no stunt work, nor did he ride in stunt cars during the show.

"B" was for Beardsley, Freddie the Freak clown. Now Freddie was a daredevil clown, rode under the car's hood on opening introduction. He also did The Pants Pull gag where the driver of a car drove up the ramp and ran his hand through a wire surrounding a newspaper Freddie was reading. The wire was attached to the top of Freddie's pants, which were made to break away, pulling the front of the pants off Freddie as he stood there. Freddie also did The Clown Slide, The Battering Ram, and Automobile Rollover or Brick Wall Crashes.

"C" for Vern "Toad" Corriel, who was a juggler, a lip-sync mimic, and a good "come-in" clown, worked the grandstand while people were entering. Toad loved grease paint, had a squeaky voice, and fit well in the show, wearing those size 28 clown shoes and a sponge ball nose. Juggling was his forte, everything including fire wands, halberds, tomahawks, rings, oranges, apples, and bananas—you name it, he's juggled it. He once told my audience that he learned juggling by watching my bookkeeper.

Vern Corriel raised a family of acrobats. He had two sons and a daughter, and did a little family act of juggling, music, and balancing, hand-to-hand, head-to-head, and that sort of thing. The Corriel family toured with us; Toad's wife was a school teacher and the kids kept sharp during their circus days and took exams when they came home and got their degrees.

Then there was Durbin, a racetrack stunting clown who also did The Pants Pull gag and The Outhouse stunt. The outhouse was built so that he could take his position in the little house set on the racetrack and a crazy motorcycle rider would come riding by and crash right through the building. The clown was hidden on a high shelf at the time of the crash and would drop to the ground while the spectators would be looking for the clown on the handlebars. The people would cast their eyes back to the house and the clown would come running out with his pants down—Sears catalogue in his hands—shaking his fist at the motorcyclist.

And there were more: Jerry Eldred, Woody Forrest, Grossi, and others through the years.

Mark my words: Never underestimate the job of a clown.

The junkers were the usual cast of characters. Old Buicks, Fords, Chevys, and the like resting heavy on their compressed springs, doors tied shut with twine, and the like.

We pulled into Honesdale at about noon before our night at the fair. The day was bright and sunny on the way to the fair, and our bill poster had covered the area telling all and sundry that this was to be the Lucky Lee Lott Hell Drivers night. He had plastered every barn, tree, and post for miles around with our red, yellow, and black posters.

Our junkers had been arranged for by my advance man. Six used cars were lined up on the infield of the racetrack, out of the way of the horse trotting races due for the afternoon entertainment. We were scheduled to set up on the track after the races and the horsemen had "winded" their steeds, which would be at about 6 pm.

The junkers were the usual cast of characters. Old Buicks, Fords, Chevys, and the like resting heavy on their compressed springs, doors tied shut with twine, and the like. Some of these old cars ran, some so-so, some poorly, and once in a while, some well. But among the junkers was one that stood a bit taller than all the others: a car called a REO, the letters derived from the initials of the inventor of the car, R. E. Olds.

This REO was a 1924 50-horsepower Model T-6, which was later known as the REO Flying Cloud. Nifty Fargo, my manager, looked it over and decided that it could be used for the feature of the night show, The Big Jump, and proceeded to de-glass it, removing the bumpers, muffler, cushions, and any other parts that were not needed as was the standard method of preparation.

After a couple of laps around the track, Fargo verified that this would be a good car and asked me to "lap it" to make sure. That I did at every date. The REO would be a fine ride for The Big Jump.

Show time, 7 pm. All the crash walls were built and in place, the ramps set in their proper places on the track, the school bus lined up for the finale, and the show was ready to go.

With the theme music, "Comedian's Gallop" on the record turntable, introduction of the performers complete, and the scheduled stunts having moved along smoothly, it was soon time for the finale.

And then one of us happened to look up at the sky. Horror of horrors, the sky was falling, with all due apologies to Chicken Little. Fog was rolling in—and fast. We were soon to be completely fogged in within a few minutes.

I signaled to the Hell Drivers to step up the pace from an already rapid-fire procedure to a machine-gun speed. For the finale, I got the REO Model T-6 in front of the grandstand, ready to belt myself in. I took a bow to the audience, and all the while continued to look up at the lowering mass of cotton. The fog cloud was about six feet above the school bus that I intended to leap over.

And as the fog lowered, the lights from the grandstand and fairgrounds increased in intensity below the density of the fog, making the scene look like something out of a fairy tale.

I usually lapped the track twice to gauge the car's feel and make sure the mechanisms were in order as well as to give the spectators an idea of what they'd be looking for when I came down the track for the finale. This night, however, as I came into the home stretch, I knew I'd never make it the second time around and so I zeroed in on the high ramps with the clouds just three feet above the top side of the bus.

I blasted off the ramps—and soared through the fog cloud. I was airborne above the fog!

In those days, I had never ridden in an airliner above the clouds, even though I had done some aerial work such as wing-walking on SPAD biplanes and the like. I'm sure that almost everyone of my readers have at some time or another ridden in airline craft and know what it is like to fly over the clouds and have had the sensation such as I experienced at Honesdale, Pennsylvania, that night.

Below me I could see nothing but fog with the lights from the fairgrounds reflected in the cotton—what an eerie sensation! Above me was a clear black sky with a full array of stars shining from the heavens.

It felt as though I had been in the air for five minutes, sailing along in my REO jump car, but reality was more like five seconds. I inevitably had to come down and when I did, I cut through the fog back into the Hell Drivers show at the fairgrounds—the fog was still at about bus top height.

I landed beautifully and flattened the catch cars. I unsnapped my safety belt and crawled out of my car—but there was no immediate applause to greet me. I strolled forward to the front of the grandstand for a bow and that was when the people realized what I'd done and then they did give me a hand. They reacted like they had seen a *real* stunt, honest to God.

My Hell Drivers told me that I had been completely out of sight above the fog cloud throughout the complete jump. I had taken off and disappeared. Except for my takeoff and landing, my jump had been invisible.

I bowed again and as I did, I looked up at the fog above the bus. The clouds were sliced clean open with a hole about ten feet wide where I had jumped up and another hole where I had come down. Through the holes you could see the stars in the clear black sky above.

The clouds were sliced clean open with a hole about ten feet wide where I had jumped up and another hole where I had come down. Through the holes you could see the stars in the clear black sky above.

The Stylish Stuntman, 1953
Yours truly ready for action with
football helmet and cravat.

CHAPTER 8

How Not to Crash an Airplane into a House

Each of the fourteen times that I crashed an airplane into a house as a daredevil stunt has left a vivid impression on my memory.

Now, contrary to what you may be thinking, The Airplane-House Crash was the simplest, easiest, most docile of all our stunts—and yet it was also the most spectacular. I was always happy to do it, happy to oblige.

And in keeping with its spectacle, it was a well-paying stunt: We pocketed $5,000 for the crash I'm going to get around to telling you about. Big money in 1941.

There was one problem associated with this stunt, however: It was an outlaw stunt. In other words, it was downright illegal to go around crashing airplanes into houses. That didn't stop us, of course. We just had to do our show and then get out of that locality faster than the Civil Aeronautics Authority could get to the site. That wasn't a problem, as you may guess: We had Hell Driver cars for the getaway.

As I wrote above, I had done The Airplane-House Crash thirteen times before this one occasion that I am now writing about. I liked airships. I didn't have a pilot's license but I was a pretty fair pilot, learned to fly by the seat of my pants fooling around out at the hometown airport with a pal who was a pilot. I had performed as a wingwalker several times and accidently done my first parachuting while wingwalking on a SPAD. That first parachute drop was without a parachute.

For The Airplane-House Crash, I used a variety of planes. Piper Cubs worked fine but the best ship was a Stearman biplane. You had to have a good, steady, strong house when you crashed a Stear-

Tri-Motor En Route, 1941
This still, taken from a 16mm movie film, shows our Ford Tri-Motor just after takeoff and on its way to our fateful Airplane-House Crash. Unfortunately, there are no photos of the actual stunt. Oh, well. A picture of the crash would just have been a blur of smoke, wood, and flying debris anyway.

Each of the fourteen times that I crashed an airplane into a house as a daredevil stunt has left a vivid impression on my memory.

man because they were tough little planes. But this occasion I am writing of is the first time I had done the stunt with anything as large as a Ford Tri-Motor.

My advance man DeLand Phillips was a sharp cookie when it came to recognizing a piece of aircraft from the baskets of bolts, nuts, pistons, cams, and cable stored in barns, sheds, and hangars anywhere in this country.

We were booked to play Rex's Fair at Amarillo, Texas, and arrived there with plenty of time on hand to survey the Panhandle. I was told that there were possible catch cars out at a town called Hartley, also in the Panhandle, where this guy junked autos, trucks, boats, and airplanes. When the word airplanes was mumbled, DeLand Phillips at my side in the driver's seat didn't wait for the informant to finish the word. We got the directions and a tank of gas and moseyed on out to Hartley and the Dry Gulch Auto Salvage.

Fellow Hell Driver Quenton Daniels from Moline, Illinois, and DeLand, who was from Madison, Wisconsin, sang merrily as they were both hooked on aircraft. The informant said the yard had at least a hundred junked aircraft and that's what my two buddies were crowing about. What with such a mother lode, I might be short two hands on the show. Some guys go for women, some for salt and pepper shakers; I had two who at least dreamed of collecting airplanes.

I left it up to DeLand to find the place. He said he could find it with his nose and that he did. The moniker Dry Gulch Auto Salvage was painted on the tops of cars in a row as we approached over a rise in the hard-packed gravel road.

Of course my DeLand didn't notice the automobiles there; all he saw were the skeletons of at least two dozen various and sundry fuselages and wing spreads. Not the whole wings, nor complete fuselage, mind you, but enough to recognize them as once having been up in the wild blue yonder. Quent didn't wait for the car to stop, but leaped out of the window of my hardtop and rattled the gate for the bearded denizen to come out of his shack to unlock the chained-up fence.

"Hard Pan Andy" came out alright, no junkyard dog, but there was a "piece" on his hip.

Before he would even approach the gate he called out, "Who sent ya?"

My credentials were, "Rex Davis, down at the Amarillo Fair."

With that he ambled over and unlocked the two padlocks and got a look at the Lucky Lee Lott Hell Drivers blazon on the side

Airplane Stunt, 1939
I loved airplanes and learned to fly by the seat of my pants at an early age although I never got a pilot's license. Here we were at the 1939 Cleveland Air Show and National Air Races with a stunt cooked up just for the show. The Piper Cub was loaded onto our car carrying the ramps, which sped along the track until we were up to enough speed for the plane to take off. The plane then circled and came in low enough to pick up a tablecloth held by a stuntman with its wingtip! Don Berry was driving the car, Dan Foley piloting the Piper, and I was on the rear bumper to stabilize the plane for takeoff.

of our car.

I filled him in on what was going on in the outside world as De-Land and Quenton were already combing those ground-bound hulks.

I'll not go into the palavering that went down between Hard Pan Andy and I. Seems that he had a car from a would-be daredevil, a Tommy somebody or other, who did air stunts and stuff along with a couple of walls or something. The guy had sold Andy the junkers after the show at the airport. It was not a successful show, he said.

Well, we didn't find a suitable airplane that day but we did get another hot lead. DeLand and Quenton couldn't find a starting point for any action on putting a plane in the air from Dry Gulch Auto Salvage, but Andy did give me a tip on where there was a Ford Tri-Motor job up in northeastern Nebraska, within miles of a

Flaming House Crash, 1939

For some strange reason, people loved to see houses crashed—especially if they were also on fire. Add layers of spills and chills, and you got great thrills. We erected a small house on the infield, filled it with wood shavings doused in gasoline, lit the whole affair on fire, and then jumped our motorcycles through it. Never fear, it wasn't as dangerous as it looks. The flames on the cycle usually extinguished themselves after a fast dash away from the scene of the crime.

Hell Driver Magazine Story, circa 1949

county fair that wanted an Airplane-House Crash so bad that my friend the fair manager could taste it. I filed the information and then went to pry my two cohorts away. We bought two clunkers for them to drive back to the Amarillo Fair after getting the flivvers started, gassed, and oiled and a round of handshakes with Hard Pan Andy.

A while later, I called on my friend Hal the fair manager up in Nebraska and told him I believed I could pull off The Airplane-House Crash that he had always dreamed of. So, we moseyed up to Nebraska to reconnoiter that Tri-Motor. We had one of the most beautiful Labor Day elements that God ever wrought. Nebraska at wheat harvest time!

I got to the location of the airplane salvage yard to make the deal that Hard Pan Andy out in Texas told me about. But there was one little hitch. As its name indicates, the Tri-Motor was powered by three engines, one on each wing and one on the nose of the fuselage. This Nebraska plane was indeed a Tri-Motor—but with only one motor left. It still had the cabin motor, but the wing motors were stripped. The lines were blocked and all that stuff as you people who are up on planes all know. The hitch was that the cabin motor alone will not lift the plane. But that sole motor will hold it in flight, so the mother of invention stepped in!

We towed the derelict to the local airport with a tether line behind my Buick Roadmaster. We did get it off the ground towing it and dropping the line in less than ten feet of altitude. I suppose the car would pull the plane down, but I doubt the plane would have lifted the car up. After some practice, Quent and I found that it took two men under these conditions to fly this tin goose. That set the stage: Quent would be inducted into his first Airplane-House Crash.

This is an occasion for you, the reader, to be able to decipher if these blurbs are on the up and up, because if you were telling me this stuff, I wouldn't believe you. But read on....

The idea was this. I would take off in the goose, circle the track and then crash the plane into a specially built house. Simple.

A "house" that I generally use for an aircraft crash is built to these specifications: 12 feet wide by 12 feet deep by 10 feet height at the eave (16 feet at the gable end) and the roof sloping front to gable and back side the same way. The corner posts of these buildings are 4x4s set in the ground 3 feet. We'd paint windows and doors visible to the spectators.

The aim of the crash is to take off and fly into the sloping side of the roof, hitting it at the eave. I fly the plane, not taxi it, at a speed of approximately 75 mph. When the plane hits the house, the prop will disintegrate, the landing gear will be ripped off, and the wings will be sent asunder. Not always, mind you, but enough so that the ship cannot fly and will not get airborne again. With the landing gear destroyed, or on World War II planes with the gear retracted, this made it a sure thing to belly in. I'd place one or two derelict cars in the plane's planned path about 100 feet beyond the house to stop it.

As is the usual procedure, I cut the power at contact, hit, and the junkman can pick up his salvage from there.

Now The Airplane-House Crash is tricky business. It has to be orchestrated perfectly—and I learned that the hard way, like everything else in life.

Occasion number one, my first Airplane-House Crash. I worked by physical signal only, and pumped just a little fuel into the goose so it wouldn't ignite post-crash. When I got into the air, my announcer began his spiel and my manager would place a bed sheet on the ground so that when the scene was set he'd lift the sheet off the ground and I'd come in.

There was one contingency to my coming in: If there was any objection to my doing the gig, he wouldn't pull the sheet. If I were to get too low on gas, I'd have to take a chance at meeting the sheriff or others and if there was any objection, that person would have

> The Airplane-House Crash was the simplest, easiest, most docile of all our stunts—and yet it was also the most spectacular. I was always happy to do it, happy to oblige.

to take possession of me while I was still in the plane. On one occasion I cut it too close and had to come in. My manager started his "Hey, rube" routine and caught the official's attention. I got out and ran across the back track, ditched my red coveralls and gave them to a guy who was fishing. I told him to run that way, I ran the other. That was my first close one.

The second time, but a year later, the ambulance tore onto the field. I broke a ketchup bag on my face, they put me into the ambulance and hauled me 30 miles to an out-of-town hospital. That was a Saturday. The officials knew they had me this time as they claimed I was not conscious when loaded into the meat wagon. The department kept a guard on my room until Tuesday and they released the driver of the ambulance. I was long gone. The driver and I had exchanged clothes on the way, ketchup and all. I never went back to that state with an airplane act after that.

Several times I had to do some maneuvering to pull the stunt. In one state they let me stay on the racetrack from the curve and I almost taxied through the house. It was illegal to fly over the people at the fair, so we had to be careful that we had the fairgrounds roped off with no one in buildings or the surrounding area.

I had never, prior to the use of that Tri-Motor, thought about going all the way through the house and continue to fly.

Getting back to the Tri (less two) Motor Ford Goose. Hal, the Nebraska fair manager, got use of the fairgrounds— not during fair time, mind you—and put our show in for a still date. He sold tickets at $3 a head for general admission and an extra $2 for grandstand, children free only if accompanied by parents. The story that it was going to be a big bird got out two days before the date. Well that sure swelled the gate, if there had been any doubt before. Twenty-two thousand people were there for that one show, which included The Airplane-House Crash. He got his money back after paying my fee and doing his advertising. The plane cost him $2,400 and the house cost $900!

The house structure for this event was somewhat different than previously described. We had to build a stronger house so it would be certain to bring down the big ship. The house was constructed around a set of telephone posts set 4 feet in the ground and extending 12 feet above ground and through the balance of the house. The house was still 12 feet deep, but ran 16 feet wide. I figured that the telephone poles would surely tear off the wings.

One other thing was different about this Airplane-House

Crash. Usually we lined up a couple junker cars to catch the plane after its slide. With the Tri-Motor we were working quick before the authorities found us so we didn't have time to find any catch cars. We were going for God's love and that's all there was to it.

For luck, I always wore red coveralls for the stunt. So before the Nebraska stunt, we headed to Sears Roebuck and got Quent fitted for his own set of red coveralls. You know, you can't find size 66 just anywhere. He was a big man, six feet five. He always made a splash with his daredevil act but being a stunt man he knew just how to roll with the punches.

On our heads we wore hard-leather football helmets for protection. We also fitted the seats with our standard getaway seatbelts reinforced with cowhide.

DeLand and Quent tuned up the Goose, reinforced the parts of the wings that had depended originally on the motor cowls for strength. We had watched the wings flapping when we brought the goose up from the graveyard and so they also ran cables from the wing tips to the wheel struts at the axle point of the landing gears. My announcer reiterated to the public that we'd pulled it all together with baling wire.

Quent and I strapped ourselves in and we towed the plane into the air behind the Buick Roadmaster. We took off with dual controls and only the imperative instruments. We came in at the house set on the infield of the racetrack from the west, heading away from the sun, naturally.

From our vantage it looked like we were smack dab on target. The house waited down there unsuspecting and we braced ourselves.

But no go. We came in just a bit too high and my prop missed the house all together. But all was not lost. We hit the target with the chin of the plane and the house disintegrated under the impact but the telephone poles didn't do their job in tearing off the wings! The undercarriage was torn off, the ailerons were shaved off, the rudder cable was destroyed, but the elevators and the wing flaps held—and we were still in the air wobbling like a turkey trying to fly. No rudder, but a heck of a lot of elevator.

We had never bothered to look at what was at the end of the racetrack because we hadn't expected to get that far. Now we saw our future directly ahead of us: A 2,700 volt high-tension wire circumventing the fairgrounds.

Quent hollered over at me, "Who in the hell put that powerline there?"

Now we saw our future directly ahead of us: A 2,700-volt high-tension wire.

Crew Chiefs, 1951
Hell Driver crew chiefs, from left:
Paul DuBoise of Detroit, Michigan;
Lucky Lee Lott; Jack Haynes of
California; and Steve Stiles of
Cayuga, Indiana.

Glad to see he wasn't too worried.

"Pull up, Quent. Pull up!" I screamed.

Quent let out a miserable, "Awk," but jerked that tree back tight.

Disappearing under our fuselage was the 2,700-volt powerline.

"Let's level," says I.

"Hell, no," interjected Quent, "got another one coming."

And so there was—2,700 more volts. I pressured down and we dove in under the second powerline. An industrial drop. Made it.

And then, right in front of us stood a house, barns, silo, and people in the yard.

I did use the sanitary facilities before I became airborne, but....

Really, kind readers, I could count the chickens running from this thing like a hawk.

"Dear God, give me a hand." I prayed.

He did.

The farmer said later that there had been an extra two rows of bricks on the chimney of his house but he didn't know what happened to them. He also said that he had brought the cows into the milk barn early so they'd be settled down come milking time. They had been in the pasture on the other side of the house where Quent and I pancaked. Didn't dive, just flat out pancaked.

After the smoke cleared, Quent said, "Give everyone my regards and we'll never do that again." We had flown 3 1/2 miles after hitting the house on the racetrack before pancaking into the pasture.

We gave the plane to the farmer's kids for a playhouse.

"Dear God, give me a hand." I prayed. He did.

CHAPTER 9

Of Mice and Motorcycle Stuntmen

Motorcycle-Car Jump, 1939
Jumping motorcycles was not so difficult. It requires just three things: Balance, bravery, and continence. This was Mickie Sullivan on one of our trusty Indian Scouts at York, Pennsylvania.

"The best laid schemes o' mice and men...," the immortal words of poet Robert Burns were running through my head the time in 1942 when we were booked at the annual St. Louis Firemen's Benefit Show.

The committee hired the Lucky Lee Lott Hell Drivers to produce the thrill show division of the combined rodeo-circus-thrill show attraction. But all was not well. A booking agent had slipped a fly into the ointment by selling the same committee an English conception of a stunt show, billed as The Greatest Attraction of the British Empire. The St. Louis newspaper reported that the English motorcycle star was the highest paid stuntman in the realm.

The Greatest Attraction could do all sorts of tricks. He rode a motorcycle while standing on the seat, while seated backwards, while standing on one shoulder, and as the finale, he was to leap over ten men and crash through a flaming board wall at the same time.

The entourage arrived the day before the opening date and included The Greatest Attraction, three roustabouts, two wives (?), and six Norton motorcycles. My crew could see that there was no way that this conglomerate of nobodies was capable of fitting into the Firemen's quality of presentation. For the Greatest Attraction's leap over ten men, he wanted my crew to lay their bodies down; his few people couldn't be put in this hazard, they said, because they were British subjects.

Over ten of my men? No way.

The *coup de grâce* came when The Greatest Attraction wanted half-inch lumber for his flaming wall crash—and then wanted it planed down to a quarter-inch thick in the center. We always used one-inch lumber in our motorcycle walls. Quarter-inch lumber

Flaming Board Wall Crash, 1939
A textbook example of our most famous motorcycle stunt. Rocky Decker assumes the correct riding position for the big moment....

Flaming Board Wall Crash, 1939
...And crashes through the one-inch thick wall and flames with nary a scratch. This was the scene at York, Pennsylvania.

Flaming Board Wall Crash, 1949
To crash through a blazing one-inch-thick board wall, you simply aimed your motorcycle, ducked your head, and rolled the throttle open. The trick was not to lift your head too soon afterward so you didn't get a splinter or two. This was Steve Stiles at Marshall, Michigan.

would burn through before the rider got to it.

Now, I've been around the block a couple times in the daredevil business and seen shows come and go, many making their exit stage left with a bruise on their noggin. In stunt driving, there are more Greatest Attractions than there are fleas on a dog, and the metaphor can be of a dual nature. I have met some of the dogs and shrugged off their parasites.

Well, the promoter of the show wasn't blind either. He paid off The Greatest Attraction and kicked him out of the arena.

The problem now facing us was that the program had already been printed extolling the deeds that the Britisher was to do. I knew one man who had worked for me on several occasions who could cut all the stuff on the printed program. We had the motor-

Tin Wall Crash, 1953
The very first Tin Wall Crash ever performed anywhere by any motorcycle stuntman! That's nothing less than 28-gauge furnace metal. The trick was to fit a sharp blade to the front wheel's fender and stake down the tin so it was as taut as possible; note the "come-along" chain holding the frame in place. This was Chuck Shue at Bethel, Ohio.

cycles with us already and materials for walls, so I got on the phone and called my old motorcycle stuntman Ron Childers to hustle on down for the opening the next night.

Ron was related to a couple of other performers who were with my show. He had shown up one day when I needed a truck driver to pull a Dodge tractor with a four-car auto transporter for one of my touring units. On the first or second day of the job, I discovered that he could ride a motorcycle like nobody's business.

I had been getting our show organized at a county fair racetrack and here comes this motorcycle with a guy standing on the seat with his arms stretched out like bird wings heading down the track at a good 40 mph. I saw it was Ron and in my mind wished him well because he was moving too fast for a tight turn that was coming up.

No problem. He made the turn alright with a little body Eng-

Hell on Two Wheels:
The Daredevil Motorcycles of Choice

With motorcycles, we went through a lot of front forks and sundry other front-end assemblies. You can probably imagine why.

I also went through a lot of motorcycles, period. I am still trying to tally them all up, but my guess is somewhere around a hundred over the years.

We typically bought our cycles from finance companies who had repossessed the bikes from their "owners." We often also picked up crashed cycles cheap from insurance companies, sorted out the good parts, and made one cycle out of two, or three, or four....

Now, I always kept my eye out for a Harley-Davidson, Milwaukee's finest, and performed many a stunt on that good Wisconsin Iron.

The best motorcycle for The Head-On Crash was a Henderson Four, which we tracked down once upon a time. The Henderson was just built well. It was something solid and dependable beneath you when you lined up against a speeding car for The Head-On.

One of my motorcycle stuntmen, Joe Langford, had an English-built Ariel Red Hunter for a time and that was a good cycle for balance acts. We also once found a 1947 Ariel Square Four up in Canada, and my riders Steve Stiles and Ron Childers used it for their acts for several years. That Ariel was a delightful machine.

But just as with Nash cars, there was one motorcycle that stood up above all others for daredevil work and that was the Indian Scout. Wall of Death Motordrome riders loved it for their circus and fair sideshows for the same reasons we did: The Scout was lightweight yet perfectly balanced. It was the ideal machine for a head stand.

Burning Tunnel Ride, 1939
Our ultimate motorcycle stunt was riding an Indian Scout through a 30-foot-long burning tunnel. There were just three essential items to complete this stunt safely: High speed, a helmet, and a leather jacket....

Burning Tunnel Ride, 1939
...And here's the front wheel of Vern Rupert's cycle emerging safely from the tunnel at Jackson, Michigan.

lish. So I watched him take another lap, this time riding on the crash bars. He was touring the track higher up on where there were deep ruts. Being in a bad position behind the handlebars and clasping the tank with his shins, he lost it. The ditch pitched him over the handlebars and smack dab into the outside hub rail, which he proceeded to take down with his shoulder.

I moved a little faster than usual and someone else called for the meat wagon. You see, there was no show going on, it was an open afternoon; we were to play that night.

The guys had a bucket of water handy that helped Ron come to. When he woke up, he didn't like the angle of his shoulder. I felt it. A slight case of dislocation, just like I had had a couple years earlier. In my case, I grabbed a post, jerked, and reset it. In Ron's case, I gave him a healthy handshake and he performed that night like a veteran. Oh, it was sore, but by this time Ron Childers was a showman.

He always itched for the chance to do a distance leap with a motorcycle. He was earning his money but wanted to do more. And the only reason he didn't get to do the distance leap—and I'm sure he could have—was that we didn't have an Indian Scout motorcycle, the only machine I ever used in leaping. The cantilever front spring is the saving grace on a leaping machine.

I digress once again. Back to St. Louis.

Ron Childers duly arrived, picked up where he would usually take over, and got the ball rolling. But the best laid plans....

On opening night, treachery was afoot. Ron was running through The Greatest Attraction's stunts with his usual class and it looked for all the world to see as if Ron was truly a great attraction. He did the numbers in the program that were worth doing or he did variations to fit his quality of stunt work.

Then came The Flaming Wall Crash.

The wall was set up and made of real one inch lumber. It was packed with excelsior wood shavings to help the wall burn and then saturated with gasoline—or whatever else had been added to the jerry cans of gasoline! We never did find what had been added to the fuel! It burst into flames like a bomb! And we never did find out who did it—but we all could guess....

Ron performed in his usual cool way. He came roaring down the track and made the jump without hesitation but his motorcycle couldn't stand the heat and he rode the rest of the way across the arena on a fireball. He laid down the burning machine and dove for cover.

We let the firemen take over from there.

> He rode across the arena on a fireball. He laid down the burning motorcycle and dove for cover. We let the firemen take over from there.

Human Jack, 1948
The kind of stunt that even bootleg bravado can't prepare you for. Here was Don "Red" Mason of Tipp City, Ohio, allowing a one-ton stake truck to run over his waist.

CHAPTER 10

Bootleg Bravado

B ootleg liquor and daredevil stunts don't mix. Beyond skewing your judgment and setting the scene for surefire disaster, the Lucky Lee Lott Hell Drivers had no need for bootleg bravado.

There were other pretenders to the stunt driving throne that were notorious drinking aficionados. And we played many a show in combination with circuses and wild west rodeos where the cowpokes had to sauce it up behind the chutes. Their bravery was dependent upon the juice.

My contract with my crew spelled out no booze. I quote: "Drinking of intoxicating liquors is out. There isn't a one of the drivers that we have hired that is a drunk and we don't want any to wind up the season being one. Consequently hard liquor is out. If any member of the crew is not a drinker don't at any time suggest that that person partake of a friendly glass. Any member of the crew who gets drunk will be fined twenty (20) bucks for the first offense, forty (40) for the second, and fired for the third." Seemed pretty clear.

Now, I didn't particularly care if the rodeo and circus stars drank just as long as it never involved my men. Drinking was something I did not allow on the job even if I was there. With the Lucky Lee Lott Hell Drivers, our drinking was done in the coffee shop.

All of this prelude stocks the stage for the time we were booked to play the Maple Leaf Gardens in Toronto, Canada, in 1943.

C anada was cold and it was wet but it was money. The promoter had arranged everything but the crawling in the car and fasten-

Hell Driver Fleet, 1953
Our army of Nash "Kenosha Kadillacs" lined up before a show.

Motorcycle Head-On Crash, 1938
Another stunt that required more than just bottled courage. Here was Whitey crashing his Henderson Four head-on into a speeding car. The car's driver could duck behind the dashboard but all Whitey could do was pretend he was a bird. Some 96,000 fans witnessed this stunt at Soldier's Field in Chicago.

ing the belt. We were booked to do our usual extravaganza with The Rollover, The Board Wall Crash, The Big Jump, and of course The Human Battering Ram.

I had hired a Canadian office executive by the name of John Pitt to do The Board Wall Crash on our Indian Scout motorcycle. John fancied himself as a star. He wore gray jodhpurs and black boots and a bright red shirt with a white tie. In fact, he wore this getup all the time—and I do mean all the time. He also had a special jacket made for himself by a sporting goods store that read "John Pitt, Daredevil—Motorcycle Stunt Man Crashing Walls." He had to use small type to get it all to fit.

Besides that, John liked to wear his crash helmet all the time as well. Our crash helmets in those days were hard leather football helmets that we got via Floyd Clymer. Well, John wore his helmet everywhere he went. This came to be a bit embarrassing so we made him take it off in the restaurant when he was with us. Pretty soon he got to picking his own cafe so he could eat in peace.

Lucky Lee and Neal Lott, 1950
Lucky Lee at 36 and brother Neal
at 30 in front of the Hell Drivers
motorized entourage. Neal handled
the Canadian Hell Drivers unit and
later started his own stunt show in
Canada.

Now John was a decent motorcycle stunt man but he was a poor choice for any other stunt. John weighed about 260 pounds and carried his own padding with him, if you get my drift. Still we needed each hand on the show to diversify a bit so John was called in to perform The Human Battering Ram.

The Battering Ram was done with a man lying prone on the hood of the car. He rode face forward with his helmeted head as the ram to burst through a wood or brick wall. The "Ironhead" placed his face on a small cushion and held on to the handles that were bolted on the side of the car.

But here we ran into a problem. Our driver, Bud Decker, who was a full six foot six, couldn't see out of the windshield because John Pitt's big posterior got in the way. That put the nix on John doing The Human Battering Ram. He was back to motorcycle stunts only.

The night of the Maple Leaf Gardens show, John ran into another problem.

The Garden in those days was strictly off limits for booze. We were working a combination Rodeo, Circus, and Thrill Show engagement, and a good number of the cowpokes had open samples of bootleg that they were passing around. The 'pokes knew our rules in the Hell Drivers but their boss figured he could stay far enough away from me that I wouldn't smell the Canadian Royale on his breath. He was wrong.

The word got around the area that the cowboys and performers were buying rotgut at $10 a flask. That brought in the Canadian Mounted Police, famed for always getting their man.

The Mounties had uniformed and plain-clothes men to guard the Queen's realm, and they were interested in the Queen's tax also. The Mountie Colonel knew that something was going on and knew that I was adverse to its going on. We had a secret meeting with the Mounties to try to work it out.

"OK, Colonel," I said, "I got an idea."

"Right 'o."

"Give me your youngest and dumbest looking man."

"I beg your pardon," quoted the Colonel.

"Alright, put it this way, have you got anyone who looks as dumb as one of my help, myself excluded?"

He was eating up the levity of it even though we were in a serious matter. "Just the man, Lieutenant Spears, twenty-three, 145 pounds, and a terrific actor. He'll play it to the hilt."

"Spears is in civvies?"

Hell Driver Crew, 1950
The 1950 season opening crew. Lower row from left: Eddie Durfee, Vic Caldwell, Steve Stiles, Al Mendanhall, and Kurt Gieske. Top row from left: our announcer "Duke" Hannaford, Nash dealer George Christie, Nash Sales Manager Stan Williamson, your servant, Lou "Batter" Crooks, and Chas. "Nifty" Fargo. Those were the days!

"Right."

"Have him go to our dressing room and suit out in one of our sets of overalls. Don't forget the rough shoes."

Spears suited up and got a little dirt on his face for cosmetics.

After he established himself as a ramp hand, he drifted toward the "head." Coming out, he was approached by a "bootie," as the Canadians called the bootleggers. Spears played reluctant, but said, "My money's in my locker, I'll have to go get it."

Spears led the way, with the bootie in tow, and went to our locker room. There were two other Mounties hiding in the locker room waiting for the money to go down. Spears took his wallet out of the locker and handed the bootie a marked Canadian tenner. And just as the bootie pocketed the bill, two Mounties appeared magically at the bootie's side and had him pinned, cuffed, and frisked before the bootie could say, "Whiskey."

Well, our problems weren't over yet.

Remember John Pitt, my motorcycle stunt man? While on the job, John was a teetotaler but any other time was his own. Trouble was, John found time for a coffee break. We had to carry all 260 pounds of him down to his hotel room. I donned his crash helmet, kickstarted the Indian Scout, and performed my best Board Wall Crash.

The show was about twenty minutes late that night but sixteen booties were picked up by the Mounties.

The Mountie always gets his man, but a little help once in a while is appreciated.

The Big Jump, 1938
The grand finale of the Chicago
Soldier's Field show featured yours
truly at the wheel of the 1936
Dodge jumping over a bus and a
lineup of catch cars. When the
smoke and debris settled, I climbed
out to take my bow.

CHAPTER 11

The Time I Lost My Hearing

Dynamite is tricky stuff. If you don't know how to use it, it's trouble. If you do know how to use it, it's a valuable tool. The Lucky Lee Lott Hell Drivers used it right in our act known as The Dynamite Drive.

The Hell Drivers' black powder man was Chick Hill, from Harrisburg, Illinois. Chick had coal mining experience in southern Illinois so he was a handy man with black powder and registered to work with it. Chick got his satisfaction out of doing a good job—a darned good job—with dynamite. In fact, he had such an attachment to this particular stunt that it almost cost him his life. In his career, he did perhaps twenty-five Dynamite Drives and each time he crawled out of the mangled messes of scrap metal with the grin of a mule in the briar patch on his face and took his bow.

We had two different ways of doing The Dynamite Drive, which we used at different times in the Hell Drivers' long career. The first was based on a simple theory—simple, albeit dangerous, as Chick learned.

Dynamite exerts its pressure downward, and if weight is placed upon it, there will be a bigger concussion, so it's best to have the sticks in such a fashion that there is no pressure at any point. In other words, suspend the dynamite off the ground. The blast will tear metal, lift hoods, burst open trunks, and rip off fenders.

In preparing a car for the first style of The Dynamite Drive, the explicit instructions were: Three sticks on the right rear frame at the bumper hanging 2 inches below the bumper; one stick at the left rear bumper but not under the fender; two sticks below the middle of the front bumper, to the right of center by about 8

Brick Wall Crash, 1938
Some of our biggest shows ever were at Soldier's Field in Chicago where we performed for 95,000 spectators on Labor Day along with a Wild West Rodeo show. Here was one of our tried-and-true staples in action. Call it hard labor: This Ford was busy breaking 2,000 bricks into small bits with the aid of twenty sticks of dynamite.

inches; and four sticks on the right frame horn and under the fender. Ten sticks in all.

The car was debrided of glass or loose accessories so that there would be no flying parts. The hood was wired down to the fenders securely. The driver rode in the driver's seat and packed himself in with padding of all sorts. The back seat of the car was padded with cushions, the front right seat was packed with cushions and any other kind of padding we could scrounge, and a roll of seat cushion padded the floorboards above the steering column.

With this style of stunt, the charge was detonated by the driver as he drove across the infield well away from man, beast, building, or vehicle. The show was spectacular with all the ripping metal you could want. But we learned our lesson. Once Chick forgot to pad himself well enough from the charge and was hauled away for repairs in the meat wagon; when the doc tried to give him a shot of morphine to ease his pain, Chick said, "No way. I've got a bad heart."

After that incident, we devised a new Dynamite Drive. Now our man would drive his car over a "minefield" planted with twelve sticks of dynamite buried in about 3 inches of sod. The dynamite was wired to a detonator, which was touched off by the passing car of the daredevil. We planted the minefield before the show and just before the act was announced, our black powder man went out and attached the battery to the detonator so that the contact of the car would finish the act.

And just like our earlier version of the stunt, the rest of the act came off easily if there was plenty of insulation, old seat cushions, styrofoam pads, and sponge rubber between the driver and the sticks of dynamite.

This was the style of act we were performing that fateful night at the Fayette County Fair at the Washington courthouse, Ohio, in 1952.

Flyer, 1947
There are no pictures of the Dynamite Car stunt in my scrapbook; perhaps everyone was covering their ears and hiding. This was a flyer sent to booking agents to promote our show. As I promised, the Hell Drivers "delivered the goods."

The Big Jump, 1941
We were back at Soldier's Field most years for Labor Day and played to monstrous crowds each time. Here I did another Big Jump in a 1938 Ford Tudor and augured into a batch of catch cars.

103

Human Jack, 1950
Hell Driver Vic Caldwell taking a
nap in the road as a 1950 Nash
goes for an afternoon drive at North
Vernon, Indiana.

I played the Fayette County Fair with my Lucky Lee Lott Hell Drivers a number of years, both before and after the Second World War. The fairgrounds was a conventional sort of park with a horse-racing track. That night it was packed with fair goers and one particular dog. Why mention man's best friend at this point? It will all come out in this treatise.

Bobby Derek was the man for The Dynamite Drive that night. Chick was having trouble with his car for the next event, The Rollover, so I told Chick to go ahead with getting his roll car running and I'd set the battery for The Dynamite Drive. Steve Stiles was on the mike.

Everything was going according to Hoyle's. We had one of our spotlights trained on the center of action and as I went out to the spot, I noticed a Dalmatian dog that no doubt belonged to one of the horsemen in the barns roaming about. I shooed the dog away and it obediently went toward the barns and stables, and I went to my post at the detonator.

At that point I should have been even more cautious than ever, but I proceeded.

We had set little white flags around the perimeter of the site locating the planted powder. It all looked OK, so I took the two ends of the detonator wire and attached them to the battery. I did not know that the detonator had already been tripped by the dog running across the line.

You already know the results. I was within 5 feet of the twelve-stick charge. The noise! The dirt! The pain!

I was jolted backwards onto my rear, blinded by the blast and struck deaf by the concussion. My face was imbedded with earth and sand and gravel. Upon contact, my shatterproof glasses gave me some protection but I never did get my glasses back as they hauled me to the Red Cross center on the grounds and then to the Washington Court House Hospital for observation.

A good eye, ears, and nose specialist took over and figured I'd live, but never go swimming or diving again. A dermatologist took a look at the flesh on my face, numbed it and finished the job of sandpapering the dirt out. It didn't hurt then, but the next day it about drove me nuts. I supposed I'd have been more ugly than what I am if that doctor hadn't done that. Call it Lucky Lee Lott's Instant Facelift Plan.

I was held for observation over the weekend, then released. I caught up with the show in Michigan.

> I was jolted backwards onto my rear, blinded by the blast and struck deaf by the concussion. My face was imbedded with earth and sand and gravel—call it Lucky Lee Lott's Instant Facelift Plan.

Nash Hell Driver, 1994
My restored 1950 Nash Statesman
painted in the colors of the Hell
Drivers.

CHAPTER 12

The Car in the Barn

Lucky Lee Lott, your faithful servant, retired from daredevilry in 1955. I promised my mother when I started the stunt car business in 1935 that I would retire when I hit forty years of age and find a safer job.

Now when a baseball player retires, he hangs up his glove. When a boxer leaves the ring, he mounts his mitts on the fireplace mantel. When the postman takes his pension from Uncle Sam, he exchanges his walking shoes for house slippers. When the ballerina quits the stage, she places her dancing slippers on a pedestal. But when the daredevil quits the car-crashing business, what has he got to enshrine for posterity?

If he's alive, that's a lot to be thankful for. Of course I have a crooked back from one too many jumps and ears that still ring from a dynamite stunt once upon a time ago.

And then there are the memories: 17,981 cars crashed, smashed, and destroyed in various other means as well as hundreds of motorcycles, fourteen airplanes, and a few dozen speedboats—all of which provide many tales for the telling.

And there are many more stories I still have to tell someday around the kitchen table. There's the time in 1956 when I was trying to establish Nash dealerships in Cuba only to be run out by Castro's revolution and escape with my life but none of my cars or cash.

And there's the time I met young Elvis Presley in 1952 when he was just breaking the ice to the big time. We were doing the famous Cotton Carnival at Memphis, and this funny looking guy in baggy pants came hightailing it down the track and said, "Mr. Lott, the Cotton Carnival manager told me to tell you that me

Back Behind the Wheel, 1994
Lucky Lee Lott at the steering wheel of his restored Nash.

Retired Daredevils, 1994
Your faithful servant in retirement
with his 1950 Nash Statesman
restored and painted in Lucky Lee
Lott Hell Drivers, colors. This car
was not originally a Hell Drivers
stunt car.

> I, Lucky Lee Lott, your faithful servant, retired from daredevilry in 1955. I promised my mother when I started the stunt car business in 1935 that I would retire when I hit forty years of age and find a safer job.

and my guys could do a 'gig' during your show a couple times today and tonight and maybe tomorrow, too." Thing was, I had no use for the guy with my show, so I turned him away. You can file that story under a chapter on "Famous People Who Knew Me."

But what about my tools of the trade? All those smashed cars live on only in the pages of my photo album with a story to be rekindled by each image. Hauled to the junkyard after each show, there was no living relic of the cars used and abused by twenty-odd years of Satan's Pals and the Lucky Lee Lott Hell Drivers.

Or is there?

And, of course, herein lies another story.

An August day in the year 1992 at my home in Tampa, Florida, affectionately known as Nashvilla. The telephone rang.

Says I, "Hello."

"Hello. Do you know a Lucky Lee Lott?" said the voice on the other end.

"This is he speaking."

"You are alive, no matter what they told me."

"Quite."

"Let me tell you something, maybe we're wasting time and you might not want to hear what I've got to say."

"Speak right up, I'll be glad to listen."

"I'm Leonard Neilson and I live a little bit south of Lincoln, Nebraska, near Beatrice, in the country. My grandfather says he saw you fly an airplane through a house up near Omaha in the 1940s, and then later your daredevils were all over Nebraska, Kansas, and Iowa. Grandad is gone but my father is still kicking and has asked me to try to find out who owns the 1952 Nash Statesman in our barn. According to the sheriff, in its day the car was never titled or licensed."

I had to get a hold on this.

He continued: "I was pretty young when you were bowling over around here. Don't recall having seen your shows but dad saw your write-up in an old auto paper a couple of years ago, it said you were from Illinois. Anyway, the man who farms our place wanted to use the old barn for machinery and asked what we were going to do with that old car out there.

"It's a pale yellow with a black top, like a taxicab. The inside is mighty dirty, the headliner is sagging to the top of the seats, and there's lettering on the doors that was either painted over or removed."

The Car in the Barn, 1992
Yours truly on the left with the 1952 Nash Hell Drivers, car found in a barn in Nebraska. I brought the car back to my Florida home and simply cleaned it up— it was in excellent condition just like the days when I first used it as a jumper car. At right is Stan Nerad of Golden, Colorado, a fellow Nash fan.

I couldn't believe my own ears. A Hell Drivers machine still among the living?

"Tell me more," I asked. "Are the tires still on it? Is it buried to its axles?"

"No, grandad put it on blocks for the first winter and it's been that way ever since."

"What was the year of the first winter?"

"That was 1952," he said. "The car is a 1952, and there is next to no mileage showing."

Then it struck home. I asked him, "Hey, is there a heavy steel plate fastened to the front bumper and another plate under the back bumper?"

"Why, yes. It is your car, right?"

"Was. The insurance company paid me for it. It was stolen over in Illinois and because it had never been registered, it was never found. What do you want for it?"

"Come on out. It's yours; you can have it."

Leonard Neilson and I kept on talking like old friends sharing the gossip.

"What were those steel plates for?" he asked.

"That one was one of our 'leaping cars.' We trailed them and never drove them cross country; that's why there was little mileage. I had fifty-nine Nashes on the road that year."

"Leonard, please tell me your trials and tribulations in finding

Football Helmet, 1992
Here I am with my old Nash jumper car wearing my original Hell Drivers football helmet. We bought these Nokona football helmets by the dozen, painted them brilliant orange, scribbled our name on the front, and strapped them on for duty. Although football helmets were never designed for daredevil crashing, they were the best choice we had at this time when car and motorcycle racers were only wearing leather aviator-type helmets. In the end, this football lid saved my life on many an occasion. *Eileen Connor*

me," I asked.

"Well, dad had read the article at some auto service venue in Lincoln and recalled that you were perhaps the same daredevil he and grandad had seen. But it wasn't until Mr. Miller asked about getting rid of the old car that we drove out to look at it."

"That was how long ago," I asked.

"When Miller was getting ready to break the ground for planting corn. April I guess. We opened the car up, trashed through the glovebox and found a yellow-and-black printed program with your picture and a little Rambler convertible up on two wheels with some other cars in the background and a list of

Crash Helmet, 1992
And here I am with a recreation of our last, true crash helmets, which I wore in the later years of the Hell Drivers. By this time, helmets were used in car and motorcycle racing and so we could buy them from several sources. Just like in the old days, we simply spray-painted them orange, slapped our stricker on the front, and got airborne.
Eileen Connor

The Legend Lives On, 1990
No, this wasn't my comeback stunt. Instead, this was a tribute show put on at the 30th Anniversary of the Sunshine Speedway in Florida. The tribute to the Lucky Lee Lott Hell Drivers was performed by Blair Nelson, who restored the 1949 Dodge in Hell Drivers' colors and built the ramps to original specifications. Here he takes off for The Flaming Board Wall Jump....

stunts inside and the name of the town in Illinois where you were from."

He had called Pekin and, in a roundabout way, finally tracked me down in Florida.

Leonard asked, "Is there any history to the car?"

"There is now," I replied. "Tell me how you, or rather your father and grandfather, came by it?" I had to find out.

"Grandfather said that a guy who worked the thrasher machine for him at thrashing time came back home in it, said he bought it at an auction in Illinois. He said he had to wait until the title got here by mail before he could drive it and so asked if he could keep it in the barn until he got straightened out."

After a bit of a pause, Leonard continued: "He died that winter in a head-on collision on the ice."

The Legend Lands Safely, 1990
...And lands on all fours. Tribute stunt driver Blair Nelson first saw the Hell Drivers as a seven-year-old boy and shook Lucky Lee's hand at the Indiana, Pennsylvania, fair.

I asked Leonard the question I was dying to know the answer to: "Did you know the name of the man who parked my car in your barn?"

Leonard gave me the name of a man who worked two weeks with the Lucky Lee Lott Hell Drivers during the 1952 season. He had been an alleged truck driver, but he would not stay off the demon sauce.

While on the road in Ohio, he ran his 48-foot-long Hell Drivers car-carrier rig into a passenger car and got himself booked for driving while intoxicated. That was it. I dropped him off the show there and then at the Greyhound bus depot with his suitcase and a one-way ticket back to his home in Lincoln, Nebraska. That was the last I ever heard of him.

Until this day.

Seems our man took himself a detour through our winter

When a boxer leaves the ring, he mounts his mitts on the fireplace mantel. But when the daredevil quits the car-crashing business, what has he got to enshrine for posterity?

quarters in our hometown of Pekin, Illinois. Parts of my show returned to winter quarters as the season wound down, and that particular year one unit was through for the season the week before Labor Day, so there were eleven cars already laid up for the winter.

Now it also seems our man still had one of the master keys that the transport drivers carried so they could load and unload show cars without looking for the assigned driver of that particular car. With key in hand, the alleged truck driver helped himself to one of my finest.

My homebase manager reported to the sheriff that a car had been stolen over a weekend. The car had no license and no registration as it was one of our jumper cars that was hauled from show to show on the kind of rig this guy used to drive.

Well, we knew who had taken the car because our man left behind an obvious clue. His Wellington boots were found on the premises alongside the space from which the car had been

116

stolen. Not a smart thief, I would venture to say.

As it came to pass, I never followed through in this matter because the insurance company paid me more for the stolen car than I had paid for it—and I had the use of the car for the season. Case closed. And long since forgotten.

The 1952 Hell Drivers Nash Statesman came home to my retirement abode later that year. It is parked in front of my house for all the world to see as they drive by on the highway.

This sole survivor has the logo emblazoned on the side marking it as one of the Lucky Lee Lott Hell Drivers cars. The car is faded and weather worn after all these years, but what would you expect, aren't we all? We earned the mantle "The World's Wildest Driver in the World's Wildest Show" the hard way. The old Hell Driver still looks ready to take off, make a few fast spins around the fairground racetrack, and leap off one of my ramps over a parked bus, land safely, and return to the grandstand for the crowd's applause.

And there's the time I met young Elvis Presley in 1951 when he was just breaking the ice to the big time. Thing was, I had no use for the guy with my show, so I turned him away. File that story under "Famous People Who Knew Me."

117

Daredevil Speak: A Compounded Fracture of the English Language

Human Jack, 1938
Variously known as The Human Jack, The Iron Man, and The Runover, this stunt scared many a mortal but was not as dangerous as it looks. That's Curly Moore as The Human Jack with yours truly at the wheel.

Advance Agent: Man who goes ahead and makes sure everything is ready.

Advertising Gee: Gimmick used in advertising.

"A" Frame Shims: Blocks used to hold the front end of a stunt car high.

Airborne: Any time the car is off the ground with all four wheels. Happened often—whether planned or not.

Approach Board: Tapered board at the bottom of a ramp for a smooth lift.

Aqua Lung: Device for doing lake jumps with safety. I needed one once.

Autobatic Driver: Newspaper idiom for stunt driver.

Banana Crate: A long double deck car hauler, holding four or five cars.

Barn Slammer: Another name for The Airplane-House Crash.

Barrel Crash: Nine barrels are stacked in pyramid fashion, set afire, and crashed.

Battery Pad: A burlap pad placed over a battery in case the car is upset.

Bicycle Wall Crash: Clown rides through a wall that is actually a set of swinging doors.

Bill Poster: A man who travels two weeks ahead to put up posters.

Blackstone (Do a "B"): Disappear without a warning.

Blindfold Drive: Driving a car with a bucket or hood on one's head.

Block Wall Crash: Concrete cinder blocks (299 of them) are stacked and the car crashes into the same, driver sits in the rear seat. On occasion the driver is in the front seat if it's a heavy car.

Blow It Up: Not what you think. Actually, it's a track command to the emcee to expand on the description of an act or kill some time while the act is getting set.

Booking Agent: An independent agent who contracts for shows.

Bottle Act: Stunt person lies on track with a bottle on head. Motorcycle rider jumps off a ramp and knocks it off (just the bottle) with the front wheel.

Breakaway Bike: Clown rides bike onto track, tears it apart and puts it back together, and rides off upside down.

Breakaway Pants: Clown standing on ramps has his pants (breakaways) pulled from his body as the driver's arm is held out

The Big Jump, circa 1954
Our apologies to the English language, but from guys who did jumps like this, it's surprising we didn't stutter our way through our words as well. This was a "You Asked For It" gig. The producer asked how many times the 1954 Ford could stand the leap. This photo showed the third leap of five.

the window catching a wire that goes around the clown's arm encircling newspaper.

Brick Wall Crash: Speaks for itself.

Bring In Basile: Track lingo for the emcee to ask the band to play. Joe Basile was Ringling's band director for years.

Bucking Phord: Rear wheels are moved forward on a clown's funny car, when passenger in rear seat moves back, car rears up.

Burger Run (Break for Steak): Sending someone to the midway or town for last-minute food all around.

Burning Privy Circuit: A string of small fairs that cannot afford a big show will get together and contract a show to play one fair one afternoon and another at night, 50–60 miles apart.

Bus Jump: You guessed it.

Buzz Barn: Building that airplane flies through.

Calliope It: We'd be waiting for the people to come into the grandstand, they were slow in leaving the midway, so we had a calliope record we'd put on the turntable and turn the volume up; that makes them "shake a leg."

Cannibalize: Take every single thing off a junker before you crash it.

Carnie Language: A language indigenous to show people that townies cannot decipher without extensive instructions. Vowels are changed to "eaz." For instance, "Mine eyes have seen" would be "Meazneaz eazziz heazveazv seazeazn."

Chicago (Do a "C"): Having worked in the film *In Old Chicago*, the drag behind the team of horses as Mr. O'Leary took his family to the city inspired the Chicago Drag stunt.

Chick Sale House: Clown goes into privy as motorcycle crashes through. Named after the writer Chick Sale who offered words of wisdom from the outhouse.

Clown Ride: Clown is shanghaied and placed in the trunk of a car for a rough ride over the ramps. He is not there after the ride.

Clown Slide: Clown is dropped from rear of car, emulating another stuntman doing the same thing—except the clown uses a grain scoop to slide on rather than the seat of his pants.

Coffee Up: Coffee pot is brewing in the tool truck—come and get it.

Day and Date: This happens when a show of some type is angered by the fact that *they* did not get to play the date we contracted. The competition will rent an empty fairground or race track and advertise that they will be there the same day and date as our show at the fair. Very rarely affects the gate for our show, but certainly cooks the goose for that so-called show ever playing this fair. I always made a point of bringing this out at the State Fair Manager's conventions. Tactics like this decimated the competition.

De-Glass: Preparing the cars for show. We did our best in keeping the horsemen and fair people happy in keeping glass and debris off the track. This term also includes removing parts of our junkers that would tend to fly off in the process of our show: bumpers, mufflers, tailpipes, cushions, and much, much more.

Dip Center Ramps: Leaping a car off a continuous flat surface often let the car jump a long distance, drop its nose thus causing an awkward nose dive. Whereas, by dipping the center of the 28-foot-long ramps, it tended to shoo the nose of the car higher into the air and consequently pancake-land the car flat.

Dive Bomber: With the advent of World War II, the word dive bomber excited the adrenalin of the spectators, so we modified our big jump by passing through about 30 feet of space striking sideways into a car placed in the path of the dive bomber. It was a higher than usual leap and shorter, but violent looking. No problems.

Door Wires: Used to hold the doors closed, thus adding strength to the structure of the car by keeping the doors closed.

Downtown De Mille: We were often called to parade, promote bond sales and other promotional action in the towns and cities as we played our dates. We called these parades our Downtown De Mille show in honor of the film director Cecil B. De Mille.

Drape the Fence: Many fairs had no control systems to hold their people from danger's way along the track. We carried several hundred feet of canvas, which we used to drape the fence and control the crowds.

Drome Riders: We mention these individuals here for they are a hardy group of midway motorcycle acrobats who often came to our bailiwick and passed the time of day with us and on occasion gave us a helping hand with one of our Indians or Harleys needing work.

Dynamite Drive: A junker is used for this stunt, wired with sticks of dynamite strapped to the undersides of the fenders, the radiator, the gas tank, some running boards, but never the hood or driver's side of the car. The car was packed with soft cushions and padding from the other cars to absorb the shrapnel of the tearing metal. The driver behind the wheel set off the charge after the car was in mid infield. Eight sticks—4 pounds—would tear off the right fenders and running boards, rip the hood off, and toss the top of the car 20–30 feet into the air, with proper preparation. Never had a man injured, except one time when the driver neglected to pack the passenger's side with padding. A mere cut on his right thigh.

Eagle: To score an eagle, that's to gain two pages of publicity or advertising in the local newspaper for one day.

Egg Gag: The egg gag consisted of the track manager cracking a bull-whip and the clown jumping at the sound of the resounding snap. The clown would lay three or four eggs on the track, the whip man would break them with one snap. On the last one, the clown said he wanted to do it too. He took a few out of his pocket, juggled them, and told the whip man he didn't need a whip and proceeded to throw them into the grandstands. They, of course, without the audience knowing it, were "nest eggs." We bought them by the gross. A nice clean clown act.

Expand the Stands: A process of getting more people into the grandstand than the authorities would allow. A few times we were hard-pressed for seating room in the stands and bleachers so we did a stunt called expanding the stands. We'd ask the person on the left aisle to keep his position and would ask the rest of the spectators on the count of three to move to their left, then again once more. One, two, three, the people were cooperative and as many as five to six hundred more people could be seated.

Express Move: Some nights we had overnighters, 400–500 miles from night to night or even afternoon shows, these jumps were made without a stop, but for dire emergency. Made one such jump from New Ulm, Minnesota, to Belleville, Kansas. Arrived in Belleville when the people were in the stands 45 minutes already. The newspaper's airplane was keeping tabs on our show as we crossed the state line coming south.

Fargo Stop Leak: In his auto polo days "Nifty" Fargo drove or rode mallet with Derby Weston in playing auto polo, which had the same rules as horseback polo. During the vicious excitement, the motors get hot and the radiators boil. So to eliminate a broken hose, the radiator hoses were replaced with sections of motorcycle tubes. In the course of this activity, these too swell and contract. A radiator sprung a leak, so to stop the leak Fargo used the handiest component on the horse racetrack, which has a swelling capacity: compressed and hardened horse manure. At a point after having stopped the leakage, the radiator hose cum motorcycle tube started to swell to the point of no return. And did it let go! Fargo and Derby rode their own merry way with their polo car strapped to the top of their 1924 Nash and not one of their compatriots would venture near them for hundreds of miles.

Fire Hoop: A hoop of lattice 6 feet across wrapped with burlap and soaked with gasoline. It is set in front of a 36-inch-high, 28-foot-long ramp, and a motorcycle is leaped through it after it is ignited.

First of May: A stuntman on his first season out.

Flaming Tunnel: A tunnel made of lattice boards, chicken wire mesh, and excelsior wood chips, then saturated with gasoline. It was ignited at which time the motorcycle rider went through the length of it. The rider continued on for about 600 feet with flaming wood chips flying behind him.

Flaming Walls: Flaming walls for cars and motorcycles to crash through were made of 1-inch yellow pine lumber staked securely to the track. For the motorcycle stunt, the walls were crossed with a 2x4 top and center, with the center on the approach side of the wall; that 2x4 breaks first and splits the rest of the boards as it goes through. The car wall jump was done from a ramp 16 inches high, 14 feet long.

Flat Rate Contract: A contract where we were hired by the fair to produce our show. The fair did the advertising, furnished us with the junkers, lumber, bricks, barrels, and any and all other materials we needed for the show. If we were rained out, we were paid the full amount anyway. The fair carried the insurance.

Flickers on the Track: Word is out that there are motion picture people taking pictures and the unit manager is to get his name and the company for future use.

Forward Spin: A car being driven in for the driver to be introduced, maneuvered by twisting the steering wheel to the left or right as the case may be, in a fashion that lets the car fantail to line it up in continuity with other cars.

Funny Car: Clown-operated car with various and sundry options to get laughs.

Get Nashing: Go to the Nash dealer.

Gillette (As in "Do a gillette"): Time to shave.

Glamor Up: Put on a uniform.

Go Juice: Starter fluid.

Goldbricker: A stuntman or helper screwing off on the job. Lazy and soon to be replaced.

Go to the Bank: Draw time.

Go to the Library: Have a date.

Grab Joint: Carnival midway eating place.

Head Job on a Coupe: Get a coupe ready for the motorcycle head-on crash by cutting off the top, top of steering wheel, and the windshield.

Head-On Crash: Two cars meet head-on in front of the grandstand. They are driven from their back seats or from the running board from which the drivers leap before hitting.

Hell Driver: *1951 Webster's Collegiate Dictionary.* "A professional stunt man. Automobile acrobat."

Hey Rube: An altercation usually instigated by a townie.

High Sides: Driving on two wheels with the right side in the air.

Hood Binder: A strap across the top of the hood to keep it from coming loose during the execution of a stunt.

Huckster: Salesman of any wares in the stands from candy to Coke to trinkets.

Human Battery Ram: Man on the hood of a car is driven through a burning wall.

Human Jack (Iron Man or Runover): Man lays down with a board on his chest and lets car or truck run over him.

Introduce Mr. or Mrs. Kalibash: Introduction of celebrity, visiting or local.

Ixnay the Agjay: Put out the cigarette.

Jack Kraft: Airplane for The Airplane-House Crash.

Jumpers: Any one of a number of cars to be used for The Big Jump finale.

Jumpers: Help that took off in the night.

Just About Bought the Farm: Seriously hurt.

Landing Cars (Crash Cars): Junkers which are used for pads.

Land Mine: Dynamite planted on the track for The Dynamite Car stunt.

Leathers: Pants, jackets, jodhpurs, breeches.

Leave Clean: Leave property so we can return.

Leave Dirty: Leave bad taste.

Left Up: Drive on two right wheels.

Lincoln (As in "Do a Lincoln"): Tear down a rail fence.

Load Out: Get ready to leave.

Lobbys: 8x10 inch photos for publicity.

Luck Charms: Trinkets to peddle.

Nash DeVille: Make bed in car, usually on the back stretch.

Natural (As in "Do a natural"): Go to the head (toilet). Can happen at unforeseen moments.

Nature and Quaker State: Term used on our CB to stop for nature and gasoline as well as water. We didn't especially want to alert gas stations in the area that a fleet was looking for a place to light.

Oil Barrel Stunt: Twenty oil drums were placed in two rows 4-feet apart in front of 16-inch-high, 14-foot-long ramps. Car lands on top of them, generally flipping over sideways. Unpredictable.

Overnight Jump: Overnight drive to make the next show on the afternoon of the next day.

Pancake: Flat landing.

Pay and Layby: Man takes time off for personal matters.

Percentage Contract: Playing for a percentage of the gate.

Pick up Pink Slips: Get titles to cars bought outright.

Pizgah: Wives.

Play Dead: Playing hurt to get into the ambulance, usually to sneak out of town.

Plug it: Talk about sponsors.

Quail: Unmarried chick. Jail bait.

Race of Death: Two motorcycle riders race to break their brick or wood wall before the other.

Railers: Troublemakers on the back stretch.

Ramps: Essential equipment to perform. We built them 28 inches wide, 14 feet long, 6 inches thick, with three 4x4 stringers and 2x6 cross pieces.

Remote Control: Clown car is driven by remote (no visible driver) control.

Reverse Spin: Car is backed up at high speed, the wheels are twisted sharply causing the car to turn around the pivot wheel.

Rollover: Run two wheels up and over 40-inch-high ramps, and twist wheels as the car leaves the end of the ramp, causing it to roll sideways.

Route Parade: If it is daylight and the show comes into town with adequate time, the entire entourage parades following the lead truck and then on to the lot.

Route Sheet: Route sheet given to each driver and car, very explicit, no east and west, always left and right. The only alternative is daylight when east and west can also be used.

Rubes and Rednecks: Troublemakers from the area.

Side by Side Stunt: Two cars working ramps at the same time.

Signing Time: Take a break to sign autographs.

Ski Jump: Any time a car becomes airborne, he is doing a ski jump.

Skid Pad: A Slide For Life man wears a skid pad on his rear proximity to slide upon.

Sleeper Cars: Before we were sponsored by Nash and could use the Nash cars that converted into beds, we had sleeper cars, which were home-rigged for sleeping in.

Slide for Life: Man drops off the back bumper and slides through a strip of gasoline set afire.

Slugs: Advertising pictures handed out to newspapers.

Sound Car: Loudspeaker car used to announce our arrival a day in advance or the day of the show if we were within 40 miles of the fair.

Split Date: Same unit plays one fair in the afternoon and another at night within 100 miles.

S S S: Shit, Shave, and Shinola. Ready for performance.

Stay on the Lot: Conditions are such that someone must stay with the equipment at all times. Don't leave the lot even to eat, send out for food.

Steeple Chase: Man or men ride on roofs of cars over ramps.

Straw Jump: Landing on straw from a Bus Jump or Big Jump.

Stretch It: Show moving too fast.

Tacker: Card-posting person.

Take it out of Granny: Change gears.

Talkers: Announcers who work the midway prior to the performance.

Ticket Palmer: Carries tickets back to be rehashed. Illegal.

Toast His Butt: Does an especially fast Slide for Life.

Track Manager: Runs the show from the track, is in charge when unit manager is in action.

Troubleshooter: Mechanic and electrician, generally riding tail car or truck in entourage.

Twenty-Four-Hour Man: Man who goes in to make sure cars are ready, especially after an overnighter.

Unit Manager: Man in charge when Lucky Lee Lott is not around.

Visit Our Money: Say nice things.

Visit Our Sponsors: Say nice things and cooperate with their suggestions.

Visit Our Townies: Say nice things.

Words of Wisdom: Safety talk given during each show.

X Parcels: Dynamite in trunk of such and such cars for cross-country hauling.

Yodeler: Bring in the musician or singer to fill in.

Index